What About Her?

A True Story Of Clergy, Abuse, Survival

Beth Van Dyke

WinePress Publishing
MUKILTEO, WA 98275

What About Her?
Copyright © 1997 by Beth Van Dyke
Published by:
WinePress Publishing
PO Box 1406
Mukilteo, WA 98275

Cover by **DENHAM**DESIGN, Everett, WA
Cover Art by Mazellan Illustration

To order additional copies please send $9.95 plus $2.95 shipping and handling to:
Beth Van Dyke
P. O. Box 17442
Irvine, CA 92623-7442
To order by phone, have your credit card ready and call
1-800-917-BOOK

Printed in the United States of America.

Library of Congress Catalog Card Number: 96-62096
ISBN 1-57921-000-7

DEDICATION

To Sean,

with love.

ACKNOWLEDGMENTS

First, I say "thank you" to my children who have faithfully stood beside me through events that have permanently affected their lives. Zan and Amber, Nicole and Rem, Jessica and Jeff, you are special gifts from God. The other precious ones who continually teach me of His love, are my grandchildren, Seth, Brian, Harrison, Allen, Christian and Erika. I love you all.

Next, I want to thank Jake, for launching me into writing. When I first began, he was to be my ghost writer. But, we were into the story only a few pages, when he said, "Beth, you need to write this story yourself. Without his strong nudging and encouragement, I would never have attempted it. Thanks for believing in me, Jake.

My deepest gratitude goes to some special people who helped me with the mundane tasks. Nancy, I appreciate the many hours you spent editing in the early stages of this book. Roy and Cecelia, thank you for helping me with the tedious line-by-line editing and reediting, making sure the final product was ready to submit for publishing. Most of all, I appreciate the way you have faithfully walked with me throughout this entire process.

There are so many others who encouraged me to write this book, even beginning way back to the early years of my recovery process. The responses of the many people who read my manuscript, let me know this was truly a story that needs to be told. This has been a long process, therefore, it would be impossible to list everyone who has given me the courage to keep on keeping on. I want to say a big "Thank You", from the bottom of my heart, to those who kept me focused on my purpose for writing this story—to reach out to the "hers" who have been forgotten.

My love,

Beth

TABLE OF CONTENTS

ABOUT THE AUTHOR

Beth Van Dyke has been married to Sean Van Dyke for 37 years. They have three grown children and six grandchildren.

She received her B.A. Degree in 1969, completed her teaching credential in 1980, and has taught public school elementary classes since that time. In 1990, she received her school district's "Teacher of the Year" Award. In 1995, she and her teammate received special district recognition for their innovative English as a Second Language Program.

Beth is currently working on a novel, based on a true story, entitled *Megan Lyn, Special Delivery*. She then wants to venture into adult fictional stories which deal with relevant issues. She also looks forward to drawing from her rich experiences as a teacher to write stories for children.

DEFINITION

WHAT IS CLERGY ABUSE?

"There are many behaviors, both verbal and physical, which can be considered sexual abuse. Professional misconduct by a person in a ministerial role includes:

* sexually suggestive discussions, comments, and innuendos
* inappropriate hugs and kisses
* intercourse
* touching of private parts (buttocks, breast, genitals) above or under clothing
* exhibitionism
* ritual abuse

"The most important consideration is, How does the religious professional's behavior make you feel? Pay attention to your feelings and trust yourself.

WHO IS VULNERABLE TO ABUSE?

"Adults, adolescents, and children may be sexually abused by people in a ministerial role. Survivors are not limited by gender; race; class; nationality; sexual orientation; or any particular religion.

"There is a power differential between people in a ministerial role and those they lead in worship, teach, supervise, and counsel. Congregants, employees, students and counseling clients are vulnerable because of the trust that is placed in the ministerial role."

CASA—Clergy Abuse Survivors Alliance

CAN THIS BE ABUSIVE TO ADULTS?

"Meaningful consent <u>can</u> <u>not</u> be given in a relationship that involves a power differential. Professional assistance is usually sought during vulnerable periods in peoples' lives. People can be taken advantage of by someone entrusted with their care."

CASSANDRA—Supporting, Advocating, Networking, Daring to Recover Association

INTRODUCTION

This story began in 1983, after a great loss interrupted my life. While I am writing a book about that loss, this personal, candid account portrays how I survived the complex dynamics that drive an inappropriate relationship between a pastor/counselor and parishioner/client. Herein lies a message of how the rippling effects of these events caused agony in so many lives.

When parishioners seek counsel from their pastor, they are susceptible to exploitation. In my case, my vulnerability was bred in an undiagnosed mental condition called Obsessive-Compulsive Disorder (OCD). However, the greatest reason which sets the stage for abuse is that the pastor is in a definite power position. Another profound power factor to the abuse equation is that he is seen as God's representative.

Perhaps this book can alert pastors, reminding them of how the enemy's deadly arrows are aimed directly toward a most strategic target -- the leaders of the flock. Because the battle is fighting the schemes of Satan, it is necessary to be clothed in the full armor of God in order to stand strong.

This story also contains a message to "the church". It must avoid denial and not excuse leaders who are in such a high calling -- leading God's flock. It is necessary for the church to hold pastors, elders and other leaders accountable.

My story comes directly from my heart to the victims, the other "hers". My prayer is that they will read my story and find courage and hope. I have risked transparency in order to help break the devastating cycle of abuse. The process is painful, but only as steps are taken to disclose secrets, can true healing be found.

Beth Van Dyke

CHAPTER 1

ENTRAPMENT

My body shook as I took a seat on the tan tweed upholstered sofa in his office. Bill Morgan, Pastor of Grace Church, sat staring at me with his captivating smile in the matching arm chair at a right angle from the sofa.

It seemed strange to actually be in his office for counseling. There were times before when I wanted to just drop in and chat, but there never was anything serious enough to take up his time.

My voice sounded weak, "I'm so afraid."

"What are you afraid of, Beth?" he asked.

"I've sunk so deep into a depression. For over a month the nightmarish thoughts have remained there constantly. I can't eat. I can't sleep. I've got to find help. I didn't know where to go; but after Sean and I discussed our options, we decided to start here. I was afraid you might be totally overwhelmed with my condition, but I decided to take the risk and come to you. If it's something you don't feel qualified to deal with, perhaps you can recommend another place." I stopped rambling and met his gaze.

He looked pleased, "I'm glad you started here, Beth. I

think I can help you. Why don't you tell me about it?"

"Well, I have these intrusive, terrifying thoughts. I fear I might do something to hurt the people I love—my children, or Sean. I'm afraid I will hit one of them, or do something to scare them away from me. I fear I'll lose control of myself. It's a horrible scenario that I see in my mind! If I did such a thing, I would be locked away. All alone. Forever. Separated from love. I feel like I'm in hell…"

I waited for his response. *Well, I hope I haven't totally blown him out of the water.* The warm look in his hazel green eyes hinted his empathy.

"Beth," he calmly responded, "you're not crazy."

"Do you think you can help me?"

"Yes, I do," he answered. "These thoughts are irrational, Beth. I know you would never do anything to harm another. It will take a few months to work with you, so I'd like to schedule weekly appointments. I'm confident I can handle your case. I also want you to know that if you feel overcome by fear, you can call me. You'll get through this, Beth."

There was a dichotomy of emotions erupting inside me. I dreaded to risk telling the "crazy" thoughts going on in my head, for fear that he would reject me. On the other hand, I found it intriguing to be with him and share the dark secrets of my mind.

As I walked out of his office, my spirit surged with hope. I thought, *There is a chance that Bill Morgan can help me find healing.* I also took comfort in the fact that he cared about me. Walking home from my appointment, my thoughts went back to Howard Whitney. He was the pastor of my church when I was a teenager. I associated the feelings I was experiencing with Bill, the same as when I was teenager relating to Pastor Whitney. When I was fourteen years old, I felt unloved by my father. I relished the nurturing love and affirmation from Pastor Whitney. I was drawn to him, but I was confused by my romantic fantasy toward him. I told myself he was old enough to be my father. Because I was young and naive, there was no way I could understand that what was happening was perfectly normal.

Pastor Whitney came on the scene as the leader of my small church when I was thirteen years old, soon after my mother's death. He was a strong, positive influence in my life at a time when I was lonely and feeling rejected. Perhaps it was his knowledge of my family's tragic story that motivated him to give me special attention, but I sensed his care.

Pastor Whitney never violated the innocent trust I had in him, the parent I longed for. Because he treated me as though I had great value, I went out of my way to do things to please him.

In those early teen years, I desperately tried to find acceptance and a sense of belonging. I began to seek friendships from peers who lacked personal confidence, friends whose negative influence added to the deterioration of my self-esteem. I was so thankful that God had sent Pastor Whitney into my life at that time. It was his words and acts of encouragement that challenged me to stay close to God.

On the walk home from my appointment with Bill Morgan, I was lost in my musings about Pastor Whitney and those vulnerable teen years. At that immature time in my life, when I believed I was nobly trying to please God, I was really yearning for parental love. God used my "pastor-parent" to thwart my walk down a destructive path. I'm sure God used my confused motives to be a good person at that young age to steer me in the right reaction. My heavenly Father had his hand on me through the human hand of Pastor Whitney.

As I continued walking, I connected those same feelings with Bill. I sensed that here was another "pastor-parent" in my life who cared for me.

By the time I reached my house I decided that I could put enough trust in Bill to get me through my terrifying fears. *He seems confident he can get me through this, so I'll trust his counsel and do all I can to follow his advice. I'll allow him to walk beside me as he leads me out of this nightmare. I saw warmth and compassion in his eyes this morning. Each time I feel the strong fear overtaking, I'll think of him. There may be hope after all!*

⚬➤➤➤⚬

I was glad no one was home when I arrived. I took a deep breath as I reclined on the sofa. I needed the solitude—the time to think.

Tired and weary, I reflected on my experiences with private battles of obsessive thoughts and depression. These bouts reached far back into my childhood. I never hinted to anyone of the torment within. During those times, I was able to mask the fears and phobias that threatened my sanity. People perceived me as happy.

In the midst of the fight for my mental wholeness, I managed to function and produce. I completed two years of college and then married Sean Van Dyke. I bore our first two children, and in their early years, I returned to college to complete my B.A. Degree. As a substitute teacher, I began my career.

During that time, Sean and I were active in church leadership. We worked with youth, music, taught Sunday School classes, and served on the board. We received one of the teens in our youth group, Evon Lovelace, into our home as the first of several foster youths who lived with us. Our lives were busy and full of meaning.

It was during the two years that Evon lived with us, seven years after Sean and I were married, that my symptoms flared. I made excuses for an inability to eat and the resulting weight loss. I retreated to bed and slept for hours, finding it an escape from the betrayal of my mind.

I was afraid to tell Sean of my struggle within, for I was sure I would be declared "insane" and locked away. Consequently, I was convinced I could never seek professional help.

One day in desperation, I picked up the telephone and dialed the number of the Christian Counseling Clinic. I did not intend actually to stay on the line. I only wanted to rehearse reaching out for help. However, when the receptionist answered, I could not put down the receiver. I made an appointment with Dr. Ford.

I was terrified to have to tell Sean I was experiencing mental problems, but I knew I could not conceal the fact I would be paying to see a clinical psychologist. So, after I tucked Zan, our five-year-old son, and Nicole, our three-year-old daughter, into bed, I cuddled next to Sean on the sofa.

I began talking. "Sean, I've made an appointment with Dr. Ford at the Christian Counseling Clinic…" As I struggled to unfold my problem, I was amazed at his compassion.

He cried when I finished. "Why didn't you trust me with this in the beginning of our marriage? Why have you suffered alone all these years?" He held me close, and we cried together.

It was such a relief actually to verbalize my symptoms to Dr. Ford, but I grasped hope when he responded with, "You are not crazy, Beth. You have obsessive-compulsive disorder. You will need to come to the clinic for treatment for at least six months."

I rationalized, *There is no way we can afford treatment now. I'd feel so guilty taking the money to do this. It would only add to my obsessions. No, I'll wait. Someday I'll go for treatment. Just opening communication with Sean has helped so much. And the doctor just told me I'm not crazy.*

Using Sean as my resource, and resting on the reassurance of the doctor, gave me temporary relief. My symptoms would flare from time to time, but I was able to limp along, always hoping someday it would all just go away.

The striking of the handmade wall clock brought me back to the present. *Here I am, thirty years later. The problem has not gone away. It has only intensified. I feel hopeless. And I still can't deal with the guilt of spending the money to see a professional counselor. Well, Bill is a professional counselor. He's working on his doctorate. Much of his ministry is counseling. And he seems confident to help me. Remember, Beth, if it doesn't work with him, then you can give yourself permission to spend the money.*

⟐

I could hardly wait until my appointment times rolled around. My anxiety level remained extremely high as the fear continued to haunt me day and night. My only glimmer of hope was knowing that I could call Bill anytime. That knowledge got me through from appointment to appointment.

My fifth appointment was memorable. Bill was trying to help me face my fears and phobias, but my thoughts kept drifting to him. *I'm bonding to Bill. I am so captured by the care I see in his eyes and smile. This whole idea of sharing my inner self with him both draws me and scares me. I feel confused and defenseless.*

At the end of that session, I stood to leave. I was surprised when Bill reached out, drew me into his arms, held me for a short time, and said, "Beth, I love you."

Excitement shot through my body. *What does he mean? What's going on? How will I handle this? I've been having such a struggle dealing with all the emotions I've been feeling toward him. Now, I am in his arms, and he's telling me he loves me.*

This time as I left his office and headed toward home, my step was light. I felt euphoric. I was a forty-two-year-old woman, but I felt like an infatuated teenager. I also realized the fear that had plagued me was taking flight. I did not realize it at the time, but I was trading one obsession for another.

❧⚜❧

Within a few weeks, my weekly appointments with Bill had taken on a life of their own. My week hinged on this anticipated hour with Bill. My primary need to deal with the obsessive fears became overshadowed by my obsessive thoughts of Bill. There was little room for anything else.

I privately searched for answers to my dilemma. I did not want to share this situation with anyone, because I did not think they would understand. I did not want to risk losing my counselor, the one in whom I had placed my hope of becoming free from my obsessions.

❧⚜❧

Early in my sessions with Bill, I realized the depth of my unfulfilled emotional void. My lack of parental love as a child caused me to yearn for that type of intimacy. I somehow sensed that dynamic was involved in my attachment to Bill, but I found it impossible to sort out. I was afraid of losing him; yet, I was also afraid of giving my feelings permission to flow in the direction they seemed to want to go. I thought, *I want to tell Bill what is going on inside me, but I'm afraid that will only deepen the emotional tie I feel with him.* On the other hand, I desperately need to talk to someone about it. I prayed, "God, isn't there some answer?"

Day and night I was haunted with the dilemma in which I felt trapped. Sean was my husband and I loved him; yet, I was attaching myself to another man.

I read a magazine article which dealt with the issue of a married woman being infatuated with someone else. It warned, *"The last person to tell your feelings is the person with whom you are infatuated. It is only setting yourself up for a trap."* But I rationalized, *What does the writer really know about my case? Bill is my counselor. I've got to tell him because he is my source of help.*

At 3:00 p.m. one Wednesday, I walked into the reception room in front of Bill's office. The aroma of his cologne permeated the entire area. Smelling the scent drew me as I experienced a sensual quickening in the pit of my stomach. I checked in with his secretary, Joyce, and then sat excitedly awaiting his beckoning. I knew I had to do something to find relief. I had experienced too many sleepless nights trying to sort through all of my emotions. I thought perhaps he really could give me constructive advice on how I could overcome my entrapment. I convinced myself. *I must tell Bill. He will help me find a way out.*

When Bill opened the door, the swishing of the air caused his fragrant cologne to permeate the breeze as he moved toward me. My heart banged within me threatening to burst out of my rib cage. I should have recognized the giant red flag warning me of destruction ahead, but I ignored it. Something deep inside compelled me. *I need him as my helper.*

I took my usual seat across from him. Looking around his neatly arranged office reminded me of the safety I felt the first time I reached out to him. I asked myself, *Am I risking safety today? I hope not. I cannot go on like this anymore. I've got to take action today.* I took a deep breath and blurted out, "Uh, Bill, there is something else I need to talk about today. It's important that I deal with this. It's hard to talk about."

"Go ahead, Beth," he reassured. "If it's something that's bothering you, you need to talk about it."

I responded, "But, it's awkward to talk about. It has to do with—I mean, my feelings toward you."

He said, "Say whatever you're feeling. This is the place where you need to talk about it."

"Well," I proceeded, searching for reactions from his countenance. It seemed he was handling the information with understanding. "Uh, I have this emotional attachment to you. I'm attracted to you, like a physical and emotional attraction; and I just don't know what to do with it. I guess I've always felt somewhat drawn toward you." I stopped talking and waited for his verbal response.

"Oh, what you're experiencing is normal," he said. I perceived a flippant overtone. "It happens all the time. The client attaches herself to the counselor. We can deal with this."

"Oh, good," I sighed. I felt relief that I had made the decision to talk to him about the problem. I continued to examine my feelings as I expressed them. "I kind of feel like you're a dad to me, a parent figure, anyway. When I was a teenager, I was attracted to my pastor. It was like an infatuation fantasy, but it was also a definite attachment with a caring, fatherlike person. He gave me a lot of personal attention—perhaps it was because he saw potential in me. Anyway, he helped me to believe in myself. He came along at a crucial time in my life. I shudder to think where I might be now if he hadn't been there to encourage me. God definitely used him to get me onto the right path."

As the session ended, I got up and moved toward the door with Bill close behind. As I turned to say goodbye, we both paused, awkwardly facing each other. My heart wanted to give him a hug. In light of the information I had just given him, I wasn't sure if it was an appropriate gesture. I just stood there waiting for some kind of signal from him. I started to turn to go, but he reached out and put his arms around me. I was confused by his warm embrace, but I rationalized. *This is a healthy expression from a helping friend.*

As I closed the office door behind me and started my walk toward home, I sensed a nagging awareness. *Something is wrong.* I tried to push it away to allow in only the feelings of elation. The dance was picking up momentum. My steps became quick and light.

I avoided Sean's eyes as I entered our home. It was my way to avoid dealing with the guilt I felt. I also wanted to stay as far away from him as possible, because I was afraid the scent of Bill's cologne would give away the fact that I had been physically close to him. I went immediately to the kitchen and grabbed the cooking utensils from the bottom cabinet. When I fumbled to open the refrigerator door to reach for the ingredients for the evening meal, I was interrupted.

"How did it go?" Sean asked. His interest was sincere; but I did not want to answer. Emotionally, I was still back in Bill's office. I only wanted to think of our embrace.

Now I was shunning the one who had always been my best friend. There was a definite estrangement unfolding between us.

Although a disastrous situation was being created, it did force some legitimate, unresolved issues in our relationship to surface. My insecurities and low self-esteem played a dynamic part in me being a passive person, especially with Sean. I had always looked to him for answers and leadership. I had a hard time making decisions, and many times I allowed Sean to make them for me. Now, suddenly, during my counsel with Bill, I started to wonder about who I really wanted to become.

Then, added to the complexity of the developing plight, was the fact that Bill always seemed threatened by Sean. Sean had been a leader in the church when Bill came on the scene at Grace Church; and rather than the two of them working together as a team, there was a competitive dynamic. It was hard to know exactly what kept them from being comfortable with each other. Sean perceived that Bill thought Sean was going to take advantage of his power or position. So, when I came to Bill for counsel and began stirring up issues in my life which needed to be addressed, Bill could not be objective. In time I realized that because Bill was not fond of Sean was reason enough for it to be the wrong place for me to receive help.

◦◦◦◦◦◦

I was both confused and excited as the inward struggle continued to churn within. Every action and thought was tainted with Bill Morgan.

Furtively, as a nervous fish darts through the water, my thoughts moved back and forth. *I feel like an infatuated teenager, but I'm a married woman! I can't feel this way, but*

I do, and I like it. This is not right! But, I can't help feeling this way. God, what am I going to do?

The dance had begun and I knew it, but I felt helpless to stop. My conscience told me the waltz was over, but in my heart the music had only begun. Beat by beat the music crescendoed. I found myself going out of my way to be noticed by Bill. I knew that he was also in step with the music.

Throughout the twenty-three years of our marriage I had been unfair to Sean because I had not been honest with him about my feelings, whenever I did not agree with him. There were reasons for that. As a child I was not allowed to express my opinions. I was taught to do what I was told with no comments or questions. I received that message through both verbal and nonverbal communication. The real message was, "You are unimportant."

In many ways I looked to Sean as a parent. I was afraid to question decisions he made concerning family matters, because I was afraid of his rejection. I also felt that he probably did know better. Nevertheless, there were times when I silently disagreed. But over the years, rather than confront, I stuffed my feelings deep inside; and resentment grew. I did not even realize it was there until I became retrospective during counseling sessions.

Hidden anger toward Sean began to surface. I started to criticize and pick apart Sean's every action. I often argued with him. As I began to emote my anger in Bill's office, a deadly dynamic began to take shape. My counselor entered into my anger directed toward Sean. We railed on him together. I rationalized that Bill just wanted to protect me; but, the truth was, Bill also had his personal vendettas to vent.

My Wednesday visits became more and more a time when I had to deal with the issue of my changing relationship with Bill. I rarely talked about my original tormenting obsessive condition, for that had been put aside. My new obsession was a bittersweet one: Bill.

As months went by my dependence on Bill grew stronger. I couldn't wait until my next counseling appointment, so I would often call him in between sessions. I knew it really wasn't counsel that I wanted as much as I wanted to be near him. Each visit almost guaranteed a hug. Before long, the hugs turned to long embraces. The holding and embracing then led to kissing. As passions flared, I knew we were venturing into areas that were dangerous and wrong, but the ecstatic excitement I felt held me captive.

೧᠁೨

One thing Bill and I shared was a common interest in the activities of the church. Because I was involved in several areas of church life, it was not uncommon for me to be there working on projects. I began using that as an excuse to be near him. It was no longer just enough to see him two or three times a week.

Bill began to express how our relationship was causing him inward unrest. One day he asked me, "Do you think our being together is in the role of counselor-client, or one of friendship? If it is friendship, what kind of friendship is it?"

"Both, I guess," I answered.

Bill contemplated and then said, "Yeah, Beth, this happens all the time in counseling. People find themselves attracted to each other. That's normal. But, you're married and so am I. I'm not going to leave my wife, and you and I are not going to ride off into the sunset together. I like you a lot, but we have to keep this in the right place. I've been reading in the book of Proverbs lately, and there are warnings there that tell me it's not wise to follow after another woman. I just need to be careful."

I could not speak. His words stabbed my heart. I did not know what caused the pain. All I knew was that it seemed unbearable. I wanted to run away from him; but I managed to say, "Yeah. You're right. Well, I'd better go." I stood and walked toward the door. I was confused when he stood up, held out his arms, and motioned for me to come to him. I responded to his beckoning when I took steps toward him. He reached out and wrapped his arms around me. We said nothing as we tightly held each other. Then he suddenly released his grip and dropped his arms at his side.

"You'd better go now," he said.

As I closed the office door behind me, I began to sob. Even though we had ventured into forbidden territory, I was devastated with feelings of rejection. I had allowed the emotional ties to wind tightly, and those ties were entangled in so many psychological dynamics. It had gone too far, but I could not handle his pulling back. I was miserable for the next two days. Saturday morning I called him. "Bill," my voice broke, "I feel terrible. I've been upset since our talk on Wednesday."

"Yeah, I've felt terrible, too."

"I feel like the harlot in Proverbs because I'm causing you to stumble," I said.

"Beth, I didn't mean to imply that. It's not you," he said. "It's me. You're a good friend, and I want our friendship to continue. Be assured that I'm still here. And, I'll continue to be. We just need to be careful."

The words and the manner in which he said them reassured me. *Bill is still my friend; so everything is going to be okay.*

He added, "We can talk more about it this week when

you come in for your appointment." There was a pause, and then he said, "Beth, I love you."

"I love you, too, Bill."

I hung up the receiver, shivering with ecstatic emotion. Sean walked into the room from the garage. He gave me a pat on my buttocks and smiled as he passed by on his way to the refrigerator. I knew he was trying to make me feel better and bring me out of my depression. I turned away from him. *It's going to be okay. Bill said it would, and he loves me.*

I churned with mixed feelings. Since Bill and I were sharing this mutual intimate problem, I allowed myself to become even more entangled in the illegitimate emotional web. I now felt closer to Bill than ever. Also, buried deep inside was my love for my husband. There were two bittersweet factors I believed. Bill cared for me, and so did Sean.

CHAPTER 2

CONFUSION

My counseling sessions with Bill started in the spring of 1983. Prior to that, we were friends and our roles were clearly defined: pastor-parishioner. Before I knew it, two years had passed. It was now the spring of 1985.

In those two years our relationship in the counseling arena grew in intensity. By the spring of 1985, I felt more and more confused. Bill and I often switched the rules and roles as we played out the game. My behavior became more and more compulsive. I constantly had to touch base with Bill. I called him, stopped by his office, and wrote him notes and letters. I needed to be reassured over and over again that he was there. Of course I did not realize it, but these behaviors were magnified symptoms of my mental disorder.

Bill's moods were unpredictable. They ranged from cold, to warm, to seductive. I never knew, from one time to the next, how he would receive me. Sometimes he greeted me with a warm hug, a tender kiss, or a kiss of passion. Other times he would be cool and reserved. When he was warm, I felt a degree of emotional stability.

Sometimes Bill seemed to turn smugly away from me as I entered his office. I perceived that he enjoyed it whenever I came to him needing his reassurance. Whenever this happened, I panicked and felt rejected. My compulsive behaviors only intensified.

I often asked myself why I subjected myself to such treatment, but the answer seemed to elude me. I knew that Sean did not play those games with me. He was always willing to affirm me. He was sensitive to my mood swings and looked out for my emotional well-being. In addition, he understood my childhood neglect and the emptiness I felt.

Sometimes, in response to my neediness, Bill would take me into his arms and hold me close. Then his hand would slip under my blouse and he would massage my back. The other hand would slide down into my pants and he would massage my buttocks. Even though I was aroused, I would gently, ever so gently, pull away. I did not want to lose him, but I would not allow him to go any further.

Somewhere buried in the quagmire of my emotions was a sensitive conscience and a loyalty to Sean. On such occasions Bill would say, "You are the strong one, Beth."

CRILLED

One of the issues I dealt with in counseling was the fact of having the great emotional hole within: the void I felt as a result of my mother's death and father's neglect. Throughout my childhood and adult years I searched to find fulfillment for that emptiness, but it was never filled. Bill counseled me that since I probably would never get my dad to respond in the way I wanted, I should develop friendships to help fill the emotional void. The first place I looked to find that needed friendship was to Bill and his wife, Pat.

Pat became one of my best friends. I liked being with her, because she was not the stereotypical pastor's wife. One of the main reasons for Pat's behavior was the fact she did not like being married to a pastor. I became one of her few confidants to whom she expressed her true feelings concerning this issue. I also found it easy to share many of my inward struggles with Pat. I enjoyed her sense of humor, and being in her presence released my freedom to laugh.

Being a friend to both Pat and Bill caused me even greater inward turmoil. My deceit and manipulation were interwoven into friendship. It was difficult for me to distinguish the basis of my motives for anything I did with either of them. Many times I asked myself, "Am I doing this for Bill, or Pat, or myself?" I could not truthfully answer that question, because I really did not know. Other times I dared not even ask myself the question.

To add to the craziness of the situation was the fact that Wendy Morgan, Bill and Pat's daughter, was my youngest daughter Jessica's best friend. The girls spent much of their time together, either at our house or at the Morgans'. Of course, that provided me with more excuses to see Bill.

I really cared for Wendy and her younger brother, Jamie. I felt guilty many times, because I did not want to betray them. I struggled with my feelings toward them, just like I did toward Pat. Again, I asked myself, "Am I doing this because I love them, or because I love Bill?"

The complexity continued to grow. Since Bill was our pastor, he officiated at our older daughter Nicole and son-in-law Rem's wedding, during the beginning stages of our entanglement. Since most of Nicole and Rem's unusual courtship happened in the "pre-Bill" era, I am thankful for the bright, golden sunshine memories of that time.

Rem lived with us for two years while Nicole was away at college. Sean and I were able to witness them risking to extend their "best bud" friendship into a love of deepest bonding and life commitment.

The wedding was a large, building-packed, happy occasion in Grace Church. Everyone who attended had anticipated the celebration, for they, too, had been intrigued by the uniqueness of their courtship. The wedding was truly a warm and cheerful event in the cold month of December.

I felt robbed of the joy that I longed for on that special day because of my obsessions with Bill. However, in spite of the dark clouds that loomed, sunbeams managed to stream through, and I drew warmth from their rays. I, the mother of the bride, was able to experience happiness for my daughter and new son-in-law.

◦⟩⟩⟩⟩⟨◦

It was not just mine and Bill's immediate families who were innocently drawn into the dynamics. So many people were drawn into the confusion of roles and relationships. Ashley Purdue was also going to Bill for counseling. Ashley was our dear friend, but more than a friend. She was our "foster daughter."

She came to us when she was eighteen years old, lacking direction and needing a place to live. She was with us several months before Sean helped her enroll in college. Although she lacked confidence and direction, we were drawn to her determination which had brought her over the tremendous obstacles in her life. She was a survivor and we believed in her.

Since Sean and I were both educators, Ashley observed first-hand the opportunities the teaching profession provided, a chance to have a positive impact on young lives while enjoying a stable income and benefits. Her problem was that she had only completed her basic high school requirements. Because she was unaware of her high academic potential, she was never channeled in the direction of a college-preparatory track.

When Ashley began checking into the possibilities of college entry, she was discouraged, feeling it would be an impossible dream. But, with her tenacious spirit, she began to work to make the impossible happen. She would not take "no" for an answer.

At the beginning of second semester, she was accepted, with a sizeable financial package, into a private college. The women's dorm provided her a place to live while she raised her sights to a belief in herself. Ashley went on to achieve her Bachelor of Arts Degree, a Colorado Teaching Credential, and then on to earn a Masters Degree. We felt honored to co-host her Master's Graduation party just days before we left for Europe. It was with great joy that we watched Ashley Purdue develop and grow over the years.

⌀〰〰⌀

Anxiety always precluded my sessions with Bill. I did not know what kind of reception to expect. One particular afternoon his mood was seductive. His habit was to lock the door after I entered, but it seemed more significant this day. After he secured the door, he inserted a tape in the cassette player. He then sat down on the sofa and motioned for me to come sit on his lap. Captured by the mood—privacy, soft music, his aroma, warmth in his eyes, and his apparent desire for me—I responded. He took me in his arms, held me close, and we kissed, first tenderly and then with passion, as though we were the only two alive. I was fully aware of our bodies and their needs to find expression, but again I backed away. I cried within. *Am I happy? Am I sad? What do I do with this desire—these feelings? God, help me!*

When I walked home that day, I did not want to talk to anyone. I was lost in the lingering thoughts and scents of Bill.

I turned the corner to my block and saw Ashley's car. *Oh, no! I forgot she's coming to dinner tonight. I don't want to talk to anyone now.* Guilt pierced my heart. *What if she finds out about Bill and me? This affair could cause her to lose her counselor. She would hate me.*

Even though on this particular night I wished that I did not have to engage myself in interacting with Ashley, I enjoyed the times she stopped by. She was like family, and I felt comfortable with her.

When I entered the house, I saw her in the laundry room folding clothes. "Hi, Beth," she said, "the dryer was beeping for someone's attention, so I decided to come to the rescue."

"Thanks so much," I said.

"I knew it was your appointment day, and I know how draining that can be. So, I decided to help you out. How did it go today?"

I hesitated. Because of our mutual counselor, many times we would discuss some of the issues we dealt with in our sessions. However, this time I did not want to discuss it. I never hinted to Ashley why it was taking months for me to "work through my problems." We both only sang praises of gratitude to our common hero counselor, Bill Morgan.

⟨⟨⟨⟩⟩⟩

Because Sean and I were both in leadership roles in the church, we were forced to interact with Bill and Pat frequently. "The Morgans and the Van Dykes" became commonly known in the church as good friends, since we were often together socially. The lines of our relationships became so entangled, that it became impossible to sort out what was legitimate interaction and what was inappropriate. Gradually, it grew into a grossly sick scene.

The lines between our roles were often blurred. The relationship between Bill and me vacillated between co-laborers, counselor-client, friend to friend, and then to two people crossing into forbidden territory.

I managed to stuff my feelings of guilt deep inside. I did not allow myself to deal with them during the greater part of our relationship. I rationalized, denied, or used whatever mechanism I could to avoid feeling guilty.

I was overly tuned into Bill's verbal and physical communication. I read into things he did as well as things he did not do. If he ever changed his usual patterns—did not sit next to me during a session, did not lock his office door, did not seem warm, or any of our other usual routines—I felt excessively insecure, thinking for sure he had emotionally left me. His unpredictable mood swings only added to my neurosis.

∽⃛∾

During one appointment he sat directly opposite me. He came across as cool and withdrawn. I tried to read him. I asked, "So…what's going on today?"

"What do you mean?" he asked as though nothing was any different than the last time he had sat down close to me and reached out to take me in his arms.

"Oh," I hesitated. "you seem to be in one of your strange moods today," I responded.

"Ah, why do you say that?" He crossed his legs as he leaned back into his chair to rest his head. His body language hinted his casual mood.

I felt foolish to tell him what I felt, but I had to talk about it. I proceeded, "Well, I noticed that you're sitting across from me today, a little different than the last time I was here."

"So," he said grinning.

"So, it seems you've moved away," I was not grinning.

"Well, I haven't."

I was not going to let him off easily. "You're acting weird today. I know something is wrong." I continued probing for reassurance. "I don't know what's wrong with me. Why do I fall apart when you do something different?"

I was even more confused when I saw a look of satisfaction cross his face. He said, "Beth, I've told you that we're special friends. I like you a lot, but I need to be very careful. I guess I've been feeling that God wants me to get my act together."

He's doing it again. On one appointment he's trying to unbutton my blouse, and then the very next time, he is quoting God and backing away. I spoke, "I want to do what God wants, too, but I also feel like an emotional yo-yo. I never know what to expect from you."

I could not hold the tears. The lump in my throat was painful. At that point, I wished the whole ordeal would just go away. There seemed no way out. "Bill," I said, "I need to end this friendship."

In anger he stood to his feet as he yelled at me, "Oh, that really solves the problem, doesn't it? Why does it have to be all or nothing with you? We can be good friends and keep from crossing over the line, Beth!"

I asked, "Where is that line, Bill?"

"Beth, you know that I'm not one to draw lines. Many things in life are in the gray zone. Things are not just black and white. Each situation is different. We just need to be careful."

"You're right," I spoke through sobs, trying to grasp his rationale, "We've got to keep this in the right place."

I stood and walked to the door. This time I reached out to embrace him. I moved my face close to his lips, but he held up his hands and backed away. He was smiling.

Feeling foolish and confused, I turned and fumbled with the door handle, trying to unlock it quickly, so that I could escape.

I walked the two blocks home feeling more rejected with each step. That evening I was beside myself as I internalized my anger and hurt. I could not eat. I waited until Sean left for a meeting, and then I called Bill at the church. *I've got to talk to someone, and he is the only one who will understand. Maybe it will help.* I froze when I heard his answering tape. I quickly hung up the receiver. I called his home. I let it ring once and then hung up. I knew if he was there, he might call back and let my phone ring once. We had never verbally planned or discussed that scheme, but it had become our signal. Two minutes later, my phone rang. Once. Then it was silent. I was once again relieved.

He is still there! Just like he said. Now I need to accept the fact that we are good friends. It's going to be okay, Beth. That one ring got me through the weekend. I kept telling myself that I was going to make it. By Sunday evening after Bible study, during which time Bill had given me no special attention with his usual glance, smile, or other signals of body language to show connection, I began having doubts again. *If I could just die, this whole ordeal could be resolved. That would be the most painless way out of all the sick relationships in this mess. It's too hard to go on like this!*

CHAPTER 3

OBSESSIONS

My compulsive behavior intensified. I was out-of-control. I had to communicate with Bill, but was frustrated as to how I could do that without being found out by either my family, or his. I went to my desk in the room that had become my office, my private domain. It was off-limits to Sean. As I emotionally crowded him out of my life, he established his own office space in an empty bedroom. This was only another symptom of our estrangement.

I started my letter to Bill.

"Dear Bill,

I do not know exactly what to say. Here
I am struggling again. I was doing so well
at feeling confident that you had not left
me—that you were still there for me..."

The door to my office opened slowly. It was Jessica. She seemed rather lonely as she stuck her head in and then entered. She said, "Hi, Mom. What's ya doin'?"

I tried to calmly shuffle papers to cover my letter to Bill and refocus my attention. "Oh, I've got some church work I need to do this evening," I lied. "What're you doing?"

"Nothin," she said, "I've been doing homework, and I'm tired of it. Just takin' a break."

"How was your day?" I asked, trying politely to make conversation with my fifteen-year-old daughter.

"It was okay." She continued to give me a rundown of some events in her day, but my mind was far away in my own world. I knew I was missing being involved in part of Jessica's life because I was so preoccupied with my own inward struggles, but I could not help myself. I wanted to cry.

Jessica left the room and I heard her turn on the TV. I nervously uncovered the letter I had started to Bill and tried to continue writing, but, in my frustration of not knowing what to write, I wadded it up and threw it in the wastebasket. I knew I had to be careful when I disposed of it, because I certainly did not want anyone to find it. It would be impossible to explain, and it could lead to a disaster. I buried it deep under other trash. I started another letter. I tore that one into pieces. I started again.

I continued my compulsive ritual. I wrote and rewrote until I came up with something acceptable. I placed it inside a book on my bookshelf so that it would not be noticed overnight. I planned to take it to Bill's office early in the morning on my way to work.

When I climbed into bed that night, I lay thinking about the letter I had written to him. My emotions were stirred, as I rehearsed in my mind each word of sentiment I had written. Then cold sweat covered my body.

I felt Sean quietly throw off the covers and get out of bed. *Is he just getting up to go to the bathroom, or is this one of those nights when he can't sleep?* The latter meant that he would be prowling around, working on one of his projects. *What if he needs to find something in the trash? He might find my rough draft to Bill.* I got out of bed, pretending that I needed a drink of water. As I passed his office door, I could see Sean writing at his desk. I turned on the water in the kitchen and then hurriedly went to the wastebasket and dug out the notes.

I was hardly able to hold them in my shaking hands as I threw them into the place I had used before for this same purpose—into the garbage disposal. I told myself that I was safe now. The evidence was gone. I lay back down. *What if Sean checks the garbage disposal before morning? I should have turned on the garbage disposal and ground up the paper, but he would have heard and wondered why I was running the garbage disposal at midnight.*

As a snowball rolls full speed down the mountain, gaining in momentum and size, so did my obsessions and compulsions. I lay there in trepidation before I finally drifted into a fitful sleep.

⟨⟨⟨⟩⟩⟩

The next morning as I got up, I continued to obsess. *Bill is going to misunderstand the letter I wrote. I came on too strong in expressing my emotions. He's going to tell me to "get lost" for sure this time.*

While getting ready for work, I wavered between delivering the letter or throwing it away. I drove to the intersection, and instead of going across Begonia Street to the church, I turned right and headed toward Eisenhower School.

Once I got into my classroom, I could think of nothing else but Bill and the letter I had labored over the night before. I wished I had taken it to him. It was forty minutes until the bell would ring, and it would be time to meet my first graders in line. I had many projects to prepare before my day of teaching, but they were overshadowed by my obsessions and compulsions.

I ran to my car, jumped in, and headed for the church. As I opened my car door to make the delivery, I anxiously reached inside my book to get the letter. There was no letter! Terror gripped my soul. I frantically searched the car. I had to find it. I talked to myself. *Calm down, you've probably left it at school.* My thoughts quickly turned to prayer. *Oh, please, God, let it be safe somewhere on my desk.*

As I drove into the parking lot, I prayed out loud, "Dear God, please help me find that letter." I got out of the car and walked toward the building. Just as I was about to step up on the curb which led to the steps in the front entrance, I looked down. Near my foot was the white envelope with the words "Bill Morgan" staring up at me. There were footprints on the envelope, but I grabbed it up and held it close. I prayed again, "Thank you, God, for looking out for me. I don't understand why you're watching out for me, but it seems you are!"

I was still shaking from the nerve racking event when I got to my classroom, and I began to rationalize once again. *Beth, you really don't have bad motives in writing to Bill. You are really stuck, and you're trying your best to work through it. It helps to express these things to Bill. He's going to help you get through this.*

With my irrational thinking, I made the decision to try again to get the letter delivered before school started. I now had twenty minutes before the bell would ring. I would not be able to get my cup of coffee from the teacher's lounge, but unless I completed this crazy mission, I would not be able to taste the coffee anyway.

Because of my position at the church as Director of Missions, I had my own key to the church office. The key also opened Bill's office door, so I cautiously unlocked his door and carefully placed the letter on his desk. I put it in my usual place—with other mail tucked inside the left side of his desk pad so that it would not look conspicuous. I ran out, afraid that Joyce might arrive early on this particular morning. I locked his door, then the office door, and escaped before anyone arrived.

The incident was typical. That morning it was only two trips. Many days I made as many as five or six going back and forth, deciding whether or not I would leave my notes. Sometimes I would deliver the note and then go back later to retrieve it, only to deliver it again. I did not realize how compulsive my behavior had become. The fact that I had to act out these rituals was only another symptom of my neurotic condition.

⟨≈≈⟩

One Wednesday in February of 1987, I sat at my kitchen table thinking about my upcoming afternoon appointment with Bill and looking at the leafless apricot tree in my backyard. This tree had always been my focus as I sat and sipped my morning coffee and contemplated my day. It had always offered me a clear sign of the seasons. Now there was no sign of life as it stood barren. I knew it was winter. *This warped relationship with Bill has been going on for three years. How long can and will it go on? I can't go on like this, but I don't want to get out of it either. I can't live with him. I can't live without him. I feel dead like that apricot tree.* It did not register that the tree was not dead; it was just sleeping.

In my musing, I thought of a day, a session when I desperately sought Bill's reassurance. He was warm and receptive. After a few minutes together, he said, "Uh, Beth, this thing between us—our friendship—that is just between you and me, okay?"

43

I was quick to answer, "Oh yes, Bill. Don't worry. You can trust me. It's just between us. I know you're hesitant to make friends, so I want you to know that you can trust me."

"I do trust you, Beth," he said. "You are one of the few people I've let into my life. I wouldn't have done that if I did not believe in your trust. You are very special."

Those final words gave me new courage to guard our secret. "No one will ever know about us, Bill," I said. "It's none of their business," I tried to convince myself more than Bill.

⟨∽⟩

By mid-April the apricot tree, that two months before seemed so cold and dead, was buzzing with life as the bees enjoyed the sweet nectar of its beautiful, brilliant pink blossoms. I was on my second cup of coffee.

I thought about the previous week. It had been a wonderful week. It was Easter vacation, and Sean and I had escaped to Palm Springs, California, for a few days of relaxing in the sun. Sean was especially tender and loving during those days, and for the first time I seriously struggled with the thought of telling Sean about the whole strange and sordid affair with Bill.

I recalled lying on the chaise lounge, watching the brilliant sunlight warm the peaceful pool. Ordinarily, I loved springtime. It was my favorite season. Before this situation, leisurely getting away with Sean to relax and bask in the early springtime sunshine was my idea of a time of perfect contentment. But, it was not like it used to be. I only felt unrest, confusion, and dread.

I looked up at the drifting, white, fleecy clouds against the azure sky. Then, I looked at Sean snoozing on the chaise lounge beside me. I thought of our upcoming summer vacation. In June, Sean and I would be leaving on an extensive vacation to visit Van Dyke relatives in Holland. We had long dreamed and planned for this trip, but now that the reality of going was near, I dreaded to leave Bill, my counselor and friend.

I panicked. I would miss him. I also needed him to help me work through the hopeless entrapment in which I found myself. I was petrified at the thought of Bill not being there. I wanted to reach out and awaken Sean. I looked at him and pretended I was talking to him. *Sean, there is so much I want to share with you. No! No! I can't.*

Seeing a beautiful butterfly land on a branch of the apricot tree brought me back from my thoughts of Easter week. *I wish I was free like that butterfly.* That momentary, peaceful image was interrupted by a troubling memory. It was the day that I casually hinted to Bill that I had thought of telling Sean "our secret."

"Beth, no. No!" He fidgeted. "That would destroy everything—the church and our families." I knew he was alarmed. "I didn't really mean it. I guess I was only saying that to get a reaction from you. Of course, I wouldn't talk to anyone about our predicament, except you, Bill. I know that would be wrong. For the sake of our families and the church, I will not tell anyone."

My mind returned from the scary memory. My eyes dropped to my cup and saucer. I prayed, "God, help me get through this mess. I love my family and friends. It would hurt so many people if they knew of what's been happening. I think also of the people I work with—the staff, my students, and parents would probably find out. It would hurt so many. Forgive me, Father, for my sin. I didn't mean to get myself in this situation. It just happened. I wasn't out looking to be unfaithful to Sean. I'm so sorry. Help me to do what's right. If I need to keep it quiet and just confess to you, then help me bear it. Help me to love Bill in the right way. I do care about him, but I feel so inadequate to handle all of this. Give me peace."

⟳▰▰◍

As time passed I only became more troubled. The guilt forced its way to the surface, and I could no longer put it down. I rationalized. I compulsively read Christian books dealing with the subject of guilt. I had to know what God wanted me to do, but I wanted to find a loophole that would salve my conscience. I tried to defend the argument that it was more loving to everyone concerned to keep it between me and God.

However, my conscience kept arguing that it would indeed be right to tell Sean. Sometimes I would look at Sean and in my mind pretend that I was telling him. *Sean, we are so far apart. We don't know each other anymore. I want to be close to your heart again—the way it used to be when we were best friends. I long for it to be that way again.*

Then I rehearsed another statement in my mind. *Sean, because I love you, I won't tell you. I will forever keep it inside.* However, that script did not bring relief.

⟳▰▰◍

Weeks went by, and I ardently wrestled with the perplexing issue as I asked myself, "Beth, what is truly the right thing to do?" I started having sleepless nights as I tossed and turned, trying to discern what God wanted me to do. I truly felt "damned if I did and damned if I didn't." There seemed no way out. I felt trapped.

I began to consider the possibility of taking my life. I told myself that it would perhaps be the best way out for all concerned. But, I was afraid God would not forgive me and I would end up in hell, forever separated from Him, the ultimate rejection! I thought of my son Zan, my

46

daughters Nicole and Jessica, my son-in-law Rem, and my little grandson Seth. I thought that although it would be devastating for Sean, he would probably be better off in the long run. I was most concerned about my children, because I remembered what it was like to experience prematurely the death-loss of my mother. I had never recovered from that. That loss was a big part of my suffering, as I tried to fill my empty love-void with Bill.

In great distress, I developed insomnia. There were nights when it seemed as though I did not go to sleep at all. I would go to work the next day in a zombie state. I had a terrifying fear that I was losing control of my body and could never sleep again. Insomnia became an obsession.

I desperately ran to Bill. He sat next to me on the sofa in his office. His presence beside me had at one time had a magnetic power, drawing me toward him. Now, his presence repelled me. The aroma of his sweet smelling cologne, which had at one time been seductive, now repulsed me. I associated its scent with guilt and sleeplessness. A gloomy cold, sweaty sensation gripped my body. Still, I could not stand to terminate our friendship. I believed I still needed him. It was too sad to walk totally away.

Whenever I suggested to Bill that I needed to get away, he would repeat, "Beth, it doesn't have to be 'all or nothing'. We can be good friends."

Sometimes before, when we went through this dialogue, I knew my motives for suggesting that I might walk away were a form of manipulation to get him to reassure me that he did not want me to walk away. It would serve its purpose, because he would become very angry whenever I told him I was going to end our friendship.

However, this time it was different. I actually started to consider the thought that I should walk away from him and never come back.

I begged him for an answer, "How do you deal with our relationship when you go home to Pat? What do you do with the guilt?"

"Well, Beth," he said, as he drew a circle on the sofa with his finger, "I just put our relationship in this circle and move it over here." He gestured to move it aside. "As far as anyone else is concerned it isn't true. They wouldn't understand, anyway."

I asked, "But what if someone in the church confronted you about us having an illicit relationship? What would you say?"

"Oh, I'd deny it," he said without hesitation. "It's in the circle. Separated. It's not true as far as they're concerned."

I was confused. However, in my desperation, I really tried to make sense of his doctrine.

Again, I hinted that I had entertained the idea of telling Sean.

"Oh, no, Beth, you can't do that," he said. "Don't you trust me?"

"Yes, Bill," I said, wanting to believe myself.

He responded, "In the night whenever you can't sleep and have doubts, I want you to stop, and in your mind listen to my voice. 'It's right that you don't tell anyone. It would destroy everything. We're going to work through this. Just trust me.'"

⟶∞⟵

The reason I went to Bill for counseling in the first place was because I was suffering from a diagnosed, but not yet understood, condition called obsessive-compulsive disorder (OCD). I did not realize it, but I had refocused my original obsessive thoughts and compulsive behaviors to Bill.

Typical of my symptoms was one night as I experienced insomnia. Falling to sleep was to no avail. I worried that I was disturbing Sean. Even though he reassured me that he could handle my restlessness, my concern for him was one more factor to keep me awake. At 1:00 A.M., I decided to make my move to the living room. I compulsively made my bed on the sofa.

Another symptom of my obsessive-compulsive condition was that my bed had to be perfect. If each sheet and blanket were not placed without flaw, I knew that would be another worry I would not be able to clear from my mind. I stared at the clock. I closed my eyes, hoping sleep would come. I started to doze into a blurry consciousness. My body jerked and I was startled. I was wide awake again.

Now, I had the sensation that I needed to urinate. I really knew I did not need to, but the only way I could clear the thought from my mind was to get up and make my trip to the bathroom. When I got back to my private bed, I had to make sure everything was perfectly in order again. I was wide awake. I tried to settle into a position that I hoped would lead to sleep. Still awake, I remembered that I did not have my lip ointment next to me. I had to moisten my lips. I repeated these same acts over and over throughout the night, but they offered no sleep.

I went through all of these rituals nightly, only to repeat them over and over until the unwelcomed sunlight would peek its looming head into my room. Underneath all of my nighttime compulsions was the unresolved dilemma, "How do I deal with the situation with Bill?"

I desperately kept seeking answers from Bill. I knew he was becoming more and more perplexed in knowing how to deal with me. The more I sensed that, the more anxious I became. I also sensed his nervousness that I really might tell the secret. I constantly kept telling him,

"You can trust me. I would never tell anyone about us. You have risked so much to help me. This is between only you and me." Saying that to him only added to my neurosis.

The hell I lived in only grew darker and darker, until there was no light. The chase I had been on, to find relief from my fears, only entrapped me in total despair. I was suffocating in the pit.

CHAPTER 4

EUROPE

As though cymbals were clashing to a deafening crescendo, summer vacation ushered in all of my mixed emotions. I was able to draw forth enough saneness to work with Sean to make last minute preparations for our long anticipated trip to Europe. Exhilaration worked its way through the disarray of clanging sounds, and I was able to look forward to seeing the countries and special places we had included in our itinerary—London, Belgium, Germany, and Holland.

It seemed like a dream. It was hard for me to believe we were actually going to see Sean's "Van Dyke" relatives in Holland. Their letters throughout the years had been so welcoming.

However, the background noise nullified my excitement. There was dread, the apprehension of being away from Bill Morgan. It will be hard to be away from Bill all summer. *I don't know if I can make it without him. Who'll be there to counsel me when I feel compelled to confess this mess to Sean? I need Bill so much! If I can connect with him in London, maybe that will help me get through the weeks to follow.*

Bill and his family had also made plans to visit London. In my fear of being left without my "counselor" and friend, I schemed to set up a rendezvous with the Morgans in London. So, it was no coincidence when the Van Dykes made reservations at the same bed and breakfast, with plans to spend a day and evening with the Morgan family. Even though I was exhausted from jet-lag, when I walked into the victorian-style entry of the Knight's Bridge Bed and Breakfast, my spirits lifted. The quaint dining room, decorated in pink floral print wallpaper, matching draperies, and china teacups and saucers on the dainty tablecloth with lavish treats awaiting weary travelers, reminded me that I truly was in another country.

However, within seconds, when I remembered that the Morgans were also registered at the same accommodation, I was surprised that some of my excitement diminished. It did not bring the comfort I had anticipated. Buried deep within the reservoir of my emotions, I wished they were not there.

Jessica brought Melissa Schultz, a school friend. Early in our plan making, Sean and I decided that since most accommodations in Europe were for two people, it would be more convenient for Jessica to have a traveling companion. Little did we realize, at that time, how important our privacy was going to be.

As both families ate the London version of an American hamburger in the Hard Rock Cafe, London, Jessica, Melissa, Wendy, and Jamie chatted and giggled as they took in all the tourist gaiety. Pat Morgan energetically chatted, as she seemed to be thoroughly caught up in her passion to experience all the grandeur of being in the venerable city that housed the royal family. Bill briefed us on the sights worth seeing while in London. Sean said little.

I sensed Sean was trying to be pleasant with people with whom he felt uncomfortable. With the mixture of jet-lag lethargy, and the awkwardness I felt being in their presence, I wanted to flee. I wanted to be alone with Sean. I thought, *When can we go back to our room? I want to lie down in Sean's arms and feel safe. I am so tired.*

"I have an idea," Pat shouted. "We haven't seen Kensington Palace yet, so let's get on the subway and go over there. Maybe we'll see Princess Diane!"

The girls chimed in, "Let's go!"

After I had fallaciously included the Morgans on our London itinerary, I found it hard to admit to them that I wanted to excuse myself and go to bed. Since the evening was still young, I felt obligated to join in some sight-seeing. I talked to myself, *Come on, Beth hold onto Sean and you'll be okay.*

"I'm game," Sean said. "I won't be good for too many hours, but I'd like to see the palace tonight. How about you, Beth?"

"I'm with you, Sean."

It was a long walk around Kensington Palace, and I was lost in my thoughts. *I can't believe I'm really here. This place is so antiquated and authentic. I wish I could enjoy and appreciate all of this. It's strange being here, and with the Morgans.*

Sean and I sat down to rest on a black wrought iron bench which decorated the magnificent landscaping. Pat and Bill went ahead to investigate their chances of getting a closer view of the palace. They disappeared for a few minutes, and then Pat came running across the lawn.

"You guys!" she yelled half out of breath, "I overheard some people say that the Queen is in town and will attend a gala celebration at the palace this evening."

She, Bill, the girls, and Jamie immediately began making plans to try to get a first-hand glimpse of the royal family later that night.

"Beth, doesn't that sound exciting?" Pat said. "Maybe we can see Queen Elizabeth tonight."

I did not hesitate to say, "Pat, I know this is a chance of a life time, but I've never felt more tired than I feel right now." I turned to Sean, "What about you?"

"No way that I'll make it," he said. "I'm ready to drop in my tracks. Besides, I'm not that impressed with the Queen and her royal fanfare. You'll have to count me out on this one."

I was so relieved that Sean did not want to go. I knew it would probably be midnight or after before they got back from their venture. I also knew I did not have the emotional energy to deal with the anxiety of being around Bill. I did not find comfort in his presence.

I found myself thinking how glad I was that I hadn't made plans to spend more than one day with the Morgans. Even though I felt anxious about being away from Bill's counseling, I was glad I would be separated from him for a few weeks. I thought, *It's good Bill, Pat, and the kids will be taking an extended vacation and won't be home for three weeks after our return.* It was halfway between consciousness and subconsciousness that the thought flashed through my mind: *I've got to get away from him!*

❦

Once we entered our room, I decided not to struggle with the strain of the evening, fight my jet-lag, or battle with the strong urge to tell Sean what was happening. Instead, I took a sleeping pill and dropped into bed. All

I wanted was for Sean to hold me securely in his arms while I fell asleep. *I will deal with life tomorrow.*

Early the next morning Sean, Jessica, Melissa, and I boarded the train headed for the Cliffs of Dover. There we boarded the jet-engined hydra-foil ferry that took us across the English Channel.

Soon after we fastened our seat belts, the loud jet engines revved. In no time, the sea vehicle lifted slightly above the water as it taxied from the channel. It felt and sounded as though we would soon be airborne as we picked up speed. The attendant, dressed in her chic navy blue uniform, announced on the intercom in broken English, "Please make yourselves comfortable. Our drip vill be approximately von hour and vivteen minutes. Ve vill zoon be coming by vid drinks and lunch…"

My heart was heavy. *If only I could fully enjoy this once-in-a-lifetime experience. I see the White Cliffs of Dover in the west, France far-off to the south, and Belgium straight ahead. I can't believe we're actually here, in between continents, just as my mind is between worlds. I wish I were free to relish it. I'm sitting here next to my husband, the one I really love. I'd give anything if this cold, fearful, sweating feeling would just go away. I want to tell Sean the whole story, but I can't. I'm so afraid it would destroy everything. I'm so desperate! God, what am I going to do?*

Throughout our ferry trip to Oostende, Belgium, my mind kept rehearsing the scene of what I wanted to tell Sean regarding my involvement with Bill. I kept telling myself, *Beth, this is crazy thinking. There is no way you can really say that to him. You've got to keep that secret within yourself for the sake of everyone.* However, my ruminations continued throughout the whole trip. I kept the scene reeling. *I cannot tell because I must protect Bill, our families, the church, and everyone else who it would affect.*

CRITLLO

There was something very romantic about the quaint sea village of Oostende, Belgium, from the moment we arrived at the "VC"—Visitor Center. From there we checked into our small hotel, and then rented the car that we would drive across the continent.

We experienced warm and friendly greetings from each person we met. In spite of my troubled soul, it felt good being there. *I don't know how I'm going to make it, but I will somehow. Maybe tonight when we're alone, I'll be able to gently tell some of this to Sean—in such a way that it won't destroy everything.*

The four of us walked around the beautiful cobble-stoned city after a pleasant dinner in the hotel. Sailing vessels were everywhere in the small harbor. The church chimes rang out, announcing it was 9:00 P.M. It seemed strange that the sun was still shining brightly in the western sky. We walked into the city centrum where Belgiumites sat at the cozy sidewalk cafes, happily chatting and sipping beer or coffee.

A city band played lively music. It was a friendly environment, and I temporarily felt euphoric. We sat down at a round table with a checkered tablecloth at one of the open cafes and joined in the celebration of a warm summer evening with sunshine. We listened to the band in the town gazebo and watched the people. Even though I knew they, too, struggled with the same universal human problems, it seemed that their life was carefree and uncomplicated. It felt good being there.

Sean said, "Look at the city square clock. It says it's 9:30. Can you believe it? It's still daylight."

I said, "I wonder what time these people go to bed. At home I'm in bed by 10:30, but I sure don't feel like it here.

My inner clock is confused. Between the jet-lag and the long evenings, it's hard to adjust, but I suppose we should head back to our hotel and try to start thinking about unwinding. We have a lot to see in Brugge before noon tomorrow."

As we walked to our hotel, I prayed. *Lord, thank you for some relief this evening. I was able to enjoy myself for a short time.* And then I resolved, *I don't know what I'm going to say, but I'm going to talk to Sean tonight.*

⟨≈≈≈⟩

It was cozy in our little room. The room had the typical soft European style twin beds, but we only needed one of them that night. We lay on Sean's bed, and I put my head on his chest. He stroked my hair. Once again I felt secure in his arms.

"Sean," I said as my heart began to pound, "I need to talk to you about my therapy with Bill."

"Okay, Beth," he said softly. "What is it?"

"Well," I cautiously began, "I don't know exactly how to say this, but…" I paused. "I've really had to struggle with feeling emotionally attached to Bill."

Sean said, "That's understandable. It's a natural thing that happens in counseling. Being a high school counselor, I've had enough experience in that area to know it just happens sometimes."

I felt relieved at Sean's understanding. I tried to accept it as a comfort to my troubled mind, but I knew I needed to continue. "It's more than just an emotional attachment. It's more like…," I fought to find the correct words—words that would explain the true situation, but that would also protect Bill. I was committed not to betray him in any way. "I guess you would call it an infatuation."

Sean said, "You mean…what you're trying to say is that you're having a mental and emotional affair with Bill."

"Yeah," I said. I was relieved that Sean said the words for me. These words did say the truth, but they also covered any involvement on Bill's part. "That's it, Sean, and I feel so guilty about it. I want you to forgive me."

"I want you to know I understand your dilemma, Beth. I do forgive you."

At that moment I felt a deep love for my husband. How many husbands would have this kind of understanding in a situation like this? I've just told him I was unfaithful to him mentally and emotionally, and he forgives me. He not only forgives me, but he understands.

That night in that quaint little room in Belgium, we held each other, talked, cried together, and loved each other. It was one of the most special and memorable times in our marriage.

It was 2:00 A.M. when we decided that we had better try to get some sleep. We needed to be ready for sight-seeing the next day. For the first time in many months, I peacefully fell asleep.

When I awoke, the glow on the hands of our traveling alarm said, "3:00 A.M.", time to make my midnight visit to the bathroom, "water closet" in Europe. As I walked down the hall, I fully awakened. Fear again overtook me. The blanket of oppression came down in smothering force. *Dear God, I've told Sean everything I can tell him. To say more would betray Bill. You know I can't do that. I felt so peaceful tonight when I told Sean my part of the involvement. I was hoping that was all that would be required of me. Is this you telling me I won't find peace until I tell him everything, or is it my own obsessive thinking? Whatever it is, I can't live with this torment! Please help me get through this vacation without risking telling it all and losing everything.*

I battled with a troubled spirit the rest of our special vacation, wanting to tell Sean all, but restraining myself for fear of "destroying everything." Most nights were spent where Sean and I talked half the night. I found it a mystery how we talked so much about my situation with Bill, yet without my telling Sean everything or his asking me to tell him everything. I cried as he stroked my head in comfort.

CHAPTER 5

RETURN TO AMERICA

By the time we returned to America, I felt a new bonding with Sean. I did not want to return home where I would have to face Bill once again and deal with all the confused emotions involving him. I wished Sean and I could simply fly away together and never return. We anticipated Nicole, Rem, and Seth's greeting at Denver International Airport, but when we saw Zan and Amber, we were shocked with excitement!

"What are you guys doing here? You're supposed to be home in San Diego."

Amber's dark brown eyes danced with a smiling mischievousness. "When Nicole and Rem told us of your plans to camp in the Rockies, we all decided to plan a big surprise for your homecoming. So, surprise! Here we are!"

I could hardly contain myself, "It couldn't be more perfect! I'm so glad we're all here! We had such a great time in Europe, but it's good we're together right now. Thank you for coming all this way to make our homecoming so special!"

Even though the heavy weight of jet-lag was crushing me, I picked Seth up into my arms and held him tightly as we walked toward the baggage claim area. *God, thank you for my grandson. He is such a joy to me in the midst of all the upheaval I'm experiencing.* I found great comfort and meaning in Seth, my first grandchild—God's precious gift.

In order to recuperate from jet-lag, our Van Dyke clan spent the first two nights in our home. The third day, we headed for the peaceful campground nestled in the quaking aspens above Golden, Colorado.

My weary heart became light and free in the four days of camping in the magnificent Rocky Mountains. My family had never seemed more important to me than they were at that time. It felt good to be back in the place where my family was of highest value.

I will always remember one particular night around our campfire. We laughed as we reminisced of happy memories. We also recalled some of the painful times. Nicole and Zan strummed their guitars and we sang. We cried. We prayed. We expressed our love to each other. God was smiling down on us, and I knew it.

I contemplated much that night as my family sat around drawing warmth from the fire. I looked at each of my children and thanked God for blessing me so abundantly.

I gazed at my daughter-in-law Amber and thought how quickly time had passed since she and Zan were married. She, like Zan, was full of adventure. That day they celebrated their first wedding anniversary by climbing a 14,000 foot peak, claiming it would definitely be a "high point" in their marriage. Their companionship contained a special quality—they both enjoyed adventures.

I loved Amber from the first. I was drawn to her tinkling laughter and striking dark eyes which danced with

energy. With her warm sense of humor and genuine compassion, I willingly opened my arms to accept her into our
family. Amber Van Dyke, the one whom people said
looked like my own daughter, truly had become one.

I pondered how Zan, with the sandy colored hair and
blue-green eyes, portrayed the Dutch characteristics of his
father. My mind went back to the time he left home. I
missed his antics that kept our home filled with laughter.
Most of all, I missed our frequent open chats. Zan's
uniqueness was his ability to win others to himself—
teachers, students, and others around him. I thanked God
that night for a son who was strong in moral character.

Jessica sat close to Zan, her big brother whom she
loved dearly. I remembered how traumatic it was for her
when he left home to go away to college. As their faces
reflected the warm glow of the campfire, I could not help
but notice their strong resemblance. Although Jessica's
hair and eye colorings were more like Sean's, I could see
another reflection of myself. Jessica, with the smiling
blue-green eyes, would always be my "baby."

When I looked at Nicole, I saw my mother.
Sometimes the flash of resemblance was so strong, it was
almost eerie; yet, I loved it. In her, I saw my mother's
reflection—her brown eyes, dark hair, body movements,
and genuine smile. As I watched Nicole throw back her
head in laughter, I clearly saw a picture of my mother,
Ramona Jackson.

While the guitars played, I watched Rem as his hazel
brown eyes gazed into the fire. Once again I was thankful
that God had brought him and Nicole together. I also felt
grateful that he was more than a son-in-law. He had
become our dear friend.

Sean, who was the anchor, a man of wisdom, was holding our grandson Seth, who was mesmerized by the fire. In

Seth, I saw a combination of Rem, Nicole, Ramona, and myself. The fire reflected the highlights of auburn in his brown wavy hair. His long eyelashes magnified his large brown eyes. As I looked at him tucked securely in his "Papa's" lap, I thought, *They mean so much to me. How did I ever become so entangled with Bill? I have risked losing all of this. They all are so special. Gifts to me from God!*

The last morning of our vacation, we were up early as we made preparations to leave. Seth had been fascinated by the fire the whole week, but since he had been carefully cautioned, he seemed to have a healthy respect for its danger. As we campers packed, rolled up sleeping bags, took down tents, and loaded our cars, Seth stayed right under our feet.

Then, when we were nearly ready to leave, we stood around the campfire for our last conversation before extinguishing the campfire. The next thing we knew Seth was falling head first into the blazing fire. In shock, we all plunged for him, but Rem, with a rush of adrenalin, was the first to grab the back of Seth's shirt to yank him out. With great force, Rem rescued his son and then held him to his breast.

With restrained cries of hysteria and trembling bodies we all surrounded Rem and Seth. We checked Seth's body for we were certain he had been badly burned. Under our careful observation, the only damage we could detect was that his long eyelashes were singed.

For the next several minutes, there was silence in our camp. Each person, in his own way, dealt with the reality of what had just happened. Rem held Seth close as he took him into the aspen forest and wept. I sat numb in shock and prayed. *Father, thank you for the miracle you just performed. I saw Seth's head in the flame, but he was virtually untouched; only his eyelashes were singed. I know his guardian angel was there with him. I don't deserve any merit from you. I'm so sorry for my sin. Help me to overcome this awful situation I'm caught in. I really do want to be free to walk close to you again. You're such a patient, loving God. I love you.*

⚬⚬⚬⚬⚬

Sean sat in the front passenger seat as he dozed. I was the lucky one to get to drive down the mountain side as we headed for home. My thoughts were racing with concerns. *I'm so relieved Bill won't be there when we get home. Knowing that it's going to be another three weeks before he arrives is a freeing thought. It feels so good being attached to Sean again. Without Bill this vacation has been such a breath of fresh air. On the other hand, I'm worried about how I will react when Bill does get back. I wish I didn't ever have to see him again. I'm so afraid for his return. I wish I could be forever released from the tormenting desire that I must tell Sean the whole story, but I know I won't have peace until it's all out. Yet, I have to think of the church, and of our families. God, please help me to have peace. Help me do the right thing.*

Sean, Jessica, and I made our rapid descent into the flat land below. The air in the Rockies had been so clear and bright. Today the Denver metropolis had a hazy overcast. I thought, *It has been such a relief to enjoy the clear, fresh air for the past few days. I hope the grayness ahead is not an omen as to how life will be when we return home.*

65

CHAPTER 6

AT THE DOOR

The Morgans would not return from their trip for three weeks. For the first time in almost four years, I enjoyed a measure of peace, as though I had returned to my "life before Bill." Sean and I resumed our responsibilities at the church. I was able to perform my duties with greater concentration and purer motives. I spent less time working on my tasks because my energies were channeled into one direction, getting the job done. Whenever I found it necessary to go to the church, I was not there to be noticed by Bill.

In the month of September, the dynamics changed once again. Bill returned. My feelings for him were stirred again. I found myself on board the merry-go-round, but this time it made me sick.

One day in early October, Bill and I sat through another session of futility. He worked on "helping me raise my self-esteem," as though that was the basis of all my problems. I sensed his desperation to help me to get control of myself. The threat of my telling our secret was growing, and I was sure he sensed it.

"Beth, I'm going to give you a homework assignment."

"Okay, and what would that be?"

He said, "I want you to think of all the positive things you do. I want you to have each member of your family write down something good about you. Bring it with you next time you come."

My guilt made it hard for me to ask my loved ones to write positive things about me. Yet, in desperation, I worked to carry out my assignment. I was determined to loose the chains of my entrapment. Throughout the week, one by one, my family members handed me their notes and letters, their complimentary comments intended to build my esteem. Sean was the last. Thursday morning came, and he still had not given me his note.

"I find it hard to give you a value list," he said. "I simply love you for who you are, not for what you do." Then he handed me a piece of paper. "But, here, I've made a list because I know it's important to you."

<hr>

I hugged the assignment to my breast as I approached the door leading into Bill's office for my 3:30 appointment. I felt such mixed emotions—attachment to Bill, an overwhelming awareness of support from my children, and a knowledge that Sean loved me. But I was not prepared for the greeting I received as I approached Bill's secretary.

While Bill stood silently at the door of his office, Joyce handed me a beautiful bouquet of red roses. The attached card read, "Beth, I love you! Sean."

I was taken back as I took the bouquet into my hands. I wanted to cry because Sean's expression meant so much. I felt awkward as I watched Bill's uncertainty as to how to react. I could not help but show excitement as I read the note from my husband. I handed my other notes to Bill, letting him know that I had taken my assignment seriously.

Once we were in his office, Bill began to silently read them, slowly and deliberately. A look of quandary came across his face. Finally, he spoke, "Beth, many people love you. You need to realize that you are a worthy person."

I left his office an hour later with my head spinning and my heart in turmoil. I knew deep inside that I had reached a turning point in my life. I knew that my family was of utmost importance. I did not know how I was going to deal with all of the entanglements with Bill, but I decided during that counseling session that my family was going to come out on top.

⊶⥲⥲⥲⥲⊷

That night I half awakened at the midnight hour. *I tried talking to myself. Stay calm. If you are really careful, you may just go back to sleep.* Just saying that woke me even more. I tried every head game I knew to try to trick myself into going back to sleep. It did not work. I was anxious. Wide awake. I knew there would be no more sleep.

This time seemed worse than anytime before. I felt I had completely lost control of my mind. I panicked. Perspiration poured from my pores. I wanted to scream, but I knew that would not solve my hopeless dilemma. I curled into a fetal ball as I sought protection. I prayed that God would take my life, but He seemed to be gone. Far away.

Hoping that I could somehow summon His presence into my room, I prayed earnestly. *God, I've got to tell Sean the whole story!* I could not breathe. I gasped for air. *This is going to be the greatest risk I've ever taken, but if I don't tell Sean before this night is over, I cannot go on living.*

Sean breathed quietly as though he might have been awake. I gingerly asked, "Sean, are you awake?"

69

"Sort of," he groggily responded, "Wanna talk?"

"Yeah, but I don't know what to say."

"Well," he patted my back. He was wide awake now and, with tenderness in his voice, he took me in his arms and said, "Just say what's on your mind, Beth!"

"I just feel so bad. There are things I need to tell you, but I can't."

"Why can't you?" he asked. "I think you need to tell me whatever it is, Beth." Sean knew the truth was more than I had told him. He had been waiting patiently for me to tell him my whole story, but in my own time. He had never probed with questions. He only held me tenderly and stroked my head.

CHAPTER 7

THE TRUTH

It was in the wee hours of the morning on that October 12th, Columbus Day. Sean said, "Beth, why don't you tell me the whole story? I really think it is time for you to get it all out."

"I can't, Sean…but I can't go on. I wish I could die."

"I know you need to tell me the whole truth, and you're afraid of my rejection," he said as though he were a mediator taking control of my protection. "Remember the bracelet I gave you last week, the one I bought for you this summer on our vacation?"

"Yes," I said, listening with anticipation of what was to follow. "I don't think I've taken it off since."

"I want to repeat right now what I told you when I gave it to you, Beth. It's a symbol of my unconditional love. Regardless of anything you've done, I love you. You've felt rejected by your family all your life. You felt you had no place you could call home, no place where you belonged. With me, you have a place just because you are. You have nothing to prove. You have nothing to earn. You are worthy.

"But," I paused and then continued, "I don't know that

you'll still accept me if I were to tell you everything."

"Why don't you tell me and let me prove my love?" he said. "Let's do it this way. I'll ask questions and you can answer 'yes' or 'no', okay?"

I dared to take the risk, "Okay."

"You said that you have been emotionally involved with Bill." He paused for a response.

"Yes."

"Was he emotionally involved with you?" Sean asked for the first time.

There was silence, and then I spoke, "Yes." I was lying on Sean's chest and could feel his heart began to pound.

He continued, "Were you physically involved?"

"Yes." I paused to take a breath, "but not really sexually."

I was sure Sean wanted to say, "Okay, just spill it all out and tell me exactly what happened," but he stayed with the script he set up.

He asked, "Did he ever kiss you?"

"Yes."

"Did he hold you in his arms?"

"Yes."

"Did he ever touch you here?" Sean touched my breasts.

A piercing pain struck my chest. "Yes...but, only through my clothing."

He continued to ask specific questions to reveal the depth of my involvement with Bill until he had a fairly accurate knowledge of the scenario. By the time he had finished asking me questions, I could tell he was shaken.

After a silence which seemed forever, Sean said, "Beth, do you realize that Bill is responsible for what has happened?"

"Not really," I said, "I think it was my fault. One day in session I told him I was attracted to him."

"That doesn't matter!" he said. "He was the counselor. You were vulnerable, and he was responsible for your well-being. Because I'm a high school counselor, I know the responsibility that goes with it. I have had so many chances to take advantage of my students, but I carefully guard their trust in me when they come to me for help. It really ticks me off that he has done this! I trusted him to counsel my wife, and he has abused that trust."

As we continued to talk, diffused light streamed through the drapes reminding us it had been another all night session. Sean would be getting up soon, but I did not want him to go.

"I'm so sorry, Sean, for what I've done," I cried. I felt such remorse.

"Beth," Sean said as he took his arms away from me. There was anger in his voice. "I'm going to have to go talk to Bill. I must confront him about this matter."

"When?" I asked. *I know I've done the wrong thing by telling Sean. Bill said if I told, it would ruin everything. I've set the wheel of the destruction in motion. Sean assured me he would love me regardless, but I know this is too much for him. Why did I tell him?*

Sean sat up on the edge of the bed. My tears turned to hysteria. He looked over his shoulder at me but did not reach for me.

"Beth," he said, "I am angry, mostly at Bill. I just need to be alone for awhile. Please try to understand that. I'm going to go to school now, and we'll talk when I get home." He paused and then said, "I do love you, Beth. I just need to be alone for awhile." He stood up and quietly proceeded to shower and prepare for school. On his way out, he bent down and kissed my forehead. "I'll see you this afternoon."

When he walked out of our bedroom, I pulled the blankets over my head. *"I want to die, God! Sean can't handle this, and I know he is leaving and may never be back. I have injured him too greatly"*

I heard the car pull out of the garage and drive away and the sound became faint and faded into silence. *Bill was right. I shouldn't have told. Now everything is ruined.*

I had been living a hellish nightmare for four years, but I never felt as hopeless as I did that morning. I lay there, curled into a ball praying to die. I felt as though my life had ended, only I was not dead. I only wished I was. *I have sleeping pills. Maybe I should take them. Is there enough to end my life? I think there are thirty pills. Maybe that would be enough. No, Beth! You can't think this way. I'm so afraid, if I did kill myself, God would reject me for sure. That would be the ultimate abandonment I've always feared.* "God," I pleaded, "Please take my life now! Please! I'm so tired of trying to live this miserable life. I want to go to be with you. God, I don't deserve your love, but please hold me close because I'm so afraid. I'm afraid of myself. I've got to quit thinking about taking my life. Please help me!"

At 11:30 that morning the telephone rang. I was still in bed drifting in and out of a fitful sleep, praying to die. My fumbling hands reached for the telephone. "Hello…" When I heard Sean's voice, I sobbed and then managed to speak, "Yes, Sean, I'm here," I heard my voice say, but it sounded distant and weak. "I'm not doing very well. How are you? I'm so sorry about all this. You must be miserable."

Sean said, "I'm coming home at noon."

"You are?" I said. "What time is it? What about school?"

He said, "I have a meeting to attend this afternoon. I

want you to go with me. Just ride along and you can sit in the car while I go to the meeting. I'm on my way now," and then he hung up.

⁂

Sean came right home and ushered me into the car. As we drove off he said, "Beth, I'm sorry I left so abruptly this morning, but I just needed space for awhile. This whole thing has really overwhelmed me. You did the right thing by telling me the whole story. That took a lot of courage. I'm extremely angry at Bill! He violated the professional code of ethics. I'm trying to decide how I'm going to deal with him. I must confront him."

"I understand," I said. "But, would you allow me to talk to him first? I betrayed him, and I want to tell him myself."

"If you feel you need to tell him yourself, yes, go ahead," Sean responded. "But remember, you did not betray him. He betrayed you by allowing this to happen in the first place."

As I sat in the car for three hours waiting for Sean, I tried to read a book to keep my mind focused away from my despair, but my mind kept coming back to the nightmare. *This can't be happening. Oh, yes! This is reality. I've really ruined everyone's life. I want to die!*

⁂

My heart was in my throat when Joyce answered the phone, "Good morning, Grace Church."

"Hello, Joyce. This is Beth, and I need to speak with Bill."

"Sure, Beth, hold on."

When Bill answered, I was direct. "Bill, it's important that I talk to you immediately."

"O-o-kay," he said cautiously. "I have an appointment now, but I can see you at 10:30."

"I'll be there."

⚬⚬⚬

I was sure he could tell from the moment I entered that I would be telling him something unpleasant.

"Bill," I did not beat around the bush, "I've told Sean the whole story." My confident facade betrayed me. A lump arose in my throat, and I could not stop the tears. "I'm so sorry."

He lowered and shook his head. "I guess I knew it was coming." He paused. "Yeah, I knew it was coming." He continued, "Now I know why Sean called me this morning to make an appointment with me this afternoon. I told him I was busy." He kept staring at the floor and then said, "Tell him I can talk to him this afternoon."

"I'll mention it to him," I said awkwardly. I knew the dance was over. I walked to the door and then stopped. I wanted to give him one last hug, not the kind I had become accustomed to. One that simply said, "Goodbye." A closure to something that should never have been.

⚬⚬⚬

I entered our tiled entry and closed the oak door behind me. I backed against it and the latch clicked. I took a deep breath and stood there. It felt good to be home.

Sean called from the den, "How'd it go, Beth? Are you okay?"

I still had not moved. "Yeah, I'm okay."

I then walked to the den and sat on the sofa close to Sean. I laid my head on his shoulder and said, "Well, Sean, Bill knows that you know everything." Then I sat up and looked into his face. "I guess it went about like I thought it would. He really didn't seem surprised. He just hung his head and stared at the floor as he shook his head. He was very distant when I walked out, but how else would he be? Oh yeah, Sean, he said he does have time to see you this afternoon. Can you see him?"

"No way!" Sean bristled. "He can wait until tomorrow afternoon. When I called him this morning to make an appointment, he didn't have time for me until tomorrow. Now that his tail is in the fire, he can find time. As far as I'm concerned, he can squirm with it until tomorrow."

Thursday afternoon Sean went to his scheduled appointment with Bill. He had been gone for over an hour, and my anxiety mounted at a rapid rate. The whole time I could not help but wonder how they were both handling the tense situation. I was concerned for Sean. I knew he was extremely angry and, although he had never done anything irrational to vent his anger, I knew this was the test of all tests. I also knew of Bill's masterful ability to use words to smooth situations and talk his way out.

One and a half hours later, Sean came barreling through the front door. I was first to speak, "How did it go?"

"Well," he said, "I was direct with him and told him how I thought he had really screwed up."

"How'd he receive that?"

"Oh," Sean said, "he was definitely apologetic. Beth, I was so angry when I went over there! I had to restrain myself from kicking in the door of his precious sports car. Then, can you believe it? When I came out of his office, I found my lawn edger had been stolen from the trunk of my car. I was so stupid to leave it in there."

"Why did you have the edger with you?" I asked.

"I had just picked it up from being repaired. I was so uptight about getting to that appointment that I figured it would be okay. After all, it was on the church property. What a joke! But, somehow, in all of this mess, the edger doesn't seem that important."

"I'm really sorry, Sean."

"Yeah, I know." He hinted a smile, "There's something in me that regrets I didn't just kick in his car door. He is so proud of that car. That would have really frosted him good."

In the intense seriousness of the situation, I also had to smile as I pictured the fantasy—Bill's perfect car with a flaw.

I continued, "He was apologetic?"

"Oh yeah," Sean said, "he accepted the responsibility for the situation. He knows he was wrong and he knows he's caught. He was squirming. I told him it was his business as to how he would deal with Pat. I said as far as I was concerned, it needed to go no further than the three of us."

"Do you think he'll tell her?" I asked.

"I really don't know what he's going to do." Sean said. "He asked me if I wanted him to resign as pastor."

"What'd you say?"

"I told him that decision wasn't going to rest on my shoulders. He'd have to think that one through himself."

I said, "I don't see how I can ever go back to that church."

"It's going to be hard, isn't it?"

Sean and I talked nonstop about Bill and the church issue for the next two hours. Then, it was as though a bolt of lightning hit him. "Beth, there is no way that Bill can stay on as pastor. I didn't want him to lay his decision to resign on me. That's his responsibility; but the more we've talked, the more I realize he must resign. He has made a gross professional error, moral and ethical, and he must leave. I just hope he sees that."

⟨⟨∽⟩⟩

Light peeked through our bedroom window, and with it came a subtle ray of peace and hope. This is the place where we had already spent hours behind a closed door as we talked, cried, reassured, soothed, and recommitted our love to each other. It was our only escape from the outside forces, ugly forces that had only begun to carry out destruction. We had no idea when I first revealed the scandalous story, how involved we would be, engulfed in such an emotional and spiritual battle. We were thankful for our place, a safe haven where we could be alone to rekindle our strength.

"Sean," I said, "You have every right to walk out on me."

"Beth," he interrupted, "I married you for better or worse."

The heavy mood momentarily gave way to lightness when a warm smile brushed across his face. "I'll admit, this does seem the worse, doesn't it?" There was silence. He looked somber. "I'm committed to you, Beth. I'm committed to our marriage. Anyway, as I keep saying to you, 'You are not responsible for what happened. Bill is.'"

"But," I said, "I think you are just saying that because you're my husband. How can you be objective? What else can you say?"

My mind flashed back to years past when my obsessive thinking was out of control. Sean would try to reassure me that I was not crazy. However, I could not accept his word. I sought objective input, an expert who would say, "You are not crazy." Now I wanted an objective expert to say, "You are not responsible for your involvement with Bill."

"Beth, it's really hard for you to accept my words, but try to believe me."

"But," I said, "I feel so guilty about it."

He said, "Okay, you've already confessed your involvement to me and God. It is right that you've done that. But, please try to see yourself as one who was vulnerable—one who sought help and got caught in something for which you were not responsible."

"I don't think others will see it that way," I said. "I wonder how the church would react to it if they ever found out."

"I don't know that they'll ever find out." Sean said, "but, if they do, I want them to know that I love you and I'm going to stand by you," Sean said.

"It's going to be hard to go to church Sunday, wondering if anyone knows, but I think we need to stand tight together," I said. "If anyone has found out, they'll know one fact, that the Van Dykes' love for each other is strong."

Sean agreed, "That's right Beth. We're going to show the church and the whole world that our marriage is going to make it, regardless of the adversity that surrounds us!"

⟨ঝৠ৹

Friday morning I called Mutual Savings to speak to Anita Kennedy. She and Pat Morgan worked in the same office, so I hoped Anita could give me a hint as to whether Bill had told Pat the news.

Also, since Anita was one of Bill's "clients" who was vulnerable and extremely dependent on Bill, I was concerned about her reaction if she found out about the truth of my relationship with Bill. There were times when I would be in Bill's office, she would call, and he would proceed to counsel her in my presence. I was flattered that he included me in his private matters, but I felt guilty of betraying Anita's trust, knowing I was in on her conversations with Bill. I felt strange when I heard him tell her some of the same words he had spoken to me, "Listen only to my voice. Do what I tell you."

Although it was not my place, I owned responsibility for Anita's well-being, since she had confidentially entrusted to me some of the troubling issues in her life. I was concerned that if she had heard of my confession, it might add enough injury to her already weakened condition to put her over the edge.

"Hi, Anita, this is Beth. How are you?...Good. Ah, this is in regard to the Missions Committee this Saturday. I am going to cancel it this time. Hope that doesn't disappoint you too much. There's just not much business to talk about right now. I'll call you later if it becomes necessary to meet." I probed, "This is Pat's day to come in, isn't it?... She left work at 9:00 this morning?... Stomach problems and crying?... Sounds like she must have been really upset.... Yeah, I know she and Bill are supposed to go away for the night with Sam and Edie. I wonder if they'll get to go."

Anita had customers and needed to go. As I hung up the receiver, I felt nauseous. Apparently Anita did not know the news, but I guessed that Pat did. I knew that when Pat was extremely upset about something, she was likely to get an upset stomach. The fact that she was crying and went home that morning, told me that it was something wrong— like perhaps Bill told her the news.

I laid on my back and stared at the ceiling. I was afraid. *Pat knows. Now Bill hates me.* As quickly as a light bulb flashes on, the tormenting obsessive thoughts forced their intrusion. *Don't you see, Beth? You are now alone. Without a counselor. Bill is gone. Forever! Your old obsessive thinking is back, and you have no one to help you now.* I panicked. I tried to think of something else. My thoughts went wild. *Remember, Beth, why you went to Bill for counseling in the first place? It was your fear that you might hurt Jessica or one of your loved ones.* The demonic thoughts seemed to jeer. *You got sidetracked, didn't you? Instantly, when you knew Bill cared for you, your obsession switched to a seduction game with Bill. You only traded one obsession for another.*

I fought to shrug the hellish thoughts from my mind, but they only grew in intensity. I lay on my bed with sweat drenching my body. I could not move. I was once again paralyzed with fear.

CHAPTER 8

CHURCH SCENE

I did not know how or why I even went to church the following Sunday. I was numb, but for some reason I was determined to go. Perhaps it was to prove that I was going to stand by my family, or perhaps it was because I was entrenched in habit. I probably was motivated by both. In spite of all the inward upheaval, it took everything in me to appear as though everything was normal.

I stood in a frozen upright position as I sang in the choir for the opening anthem. I looked out over the congregation and felt as though I were outside of my body looking in on an ominous scene. The first thing I noticed was that Pat was absent. Bill was in his usual place, seated on the front row of pews facing the choir. He looked somber with his eyes straight ahead as though looking into space. I looked over at Sean playing the piano and thought, *He is playing with extra energy this morning.* Then I saw Edie Landen. Her eyes were fixed directly on me, and they did not move. I looked away and then glanced back at her. Her penetrating eyes still stared.

God, I want to get out of this choir loft. I want to be off this stage and sitting next to Sean. No. I want to be far away from this place. Edie knows. I'll bet Pat and Bill have told Edie and Sam everything! Now that they know, it's likely to become public information.

~~~~~~

That afternoon Sean wasted no time in contacting Bill. He picked up the telephone and dialed the church number. Bill answered.

Sean spoke, "Bill. This is Sean. Beth has been upset all afternoon because she thinks Edie knows. She could tell by the way Edie stared at her all through the service. You know that since it's gone outside our families, it's going to become public information..."

Sean slowly hung up the phone and somberly turned to me. "You're right, Beth, Edie Landen does know. Bill told Pat the night that I confronted him. I guess she was quite upset, to say the least. She got right on the phone and called Edie. They went to see Sam and Edie that same evening. Bill and Pat swore them to secrecy, and then told them their story."

"Swore them to secrecy!" I yelled. "The whole church is going to find out."

"Bill stated," Sean said, "that he and Pat did go away with the Landens overnight. He said they did nothing but discuss the situation. Bill has decided to resign from the church and go to school full time to finish his doctorate. Pat is going to finance him through school since she is making a good income. They'll work on mending their marriage."

I began to cry. "He was right. I should never have told. It is destroying everything!"

◯⟳⟳⟳◯

As soon as I knew Bill and Pat had told Edie and Sam, I immediately called Nicole and Rem. I knew the word would get out, and I certainly wanted to be the one to tell my daughter and son-in-law. I said to Nicole, "Are you going to be home? Your Dad and I need to talk to you. We'll be right over."

As we entered their home, I saw anxious questions on Nicole and Rem's faces as Sean and I took our seats on the sofa. Nicole had observed my apparent depression in the previous weeks and months, and had tried to help me "fix it," yet felt helpless. Rem had so faithfully stood by and extended encouragement.

It wrenched my heart to verbalize the scenario of my entrapment with Bill. I felt naked and exposed as I flashed light on the secrets that had been covered in darkness for so long. I feared the ramifications of their disillusionment with those they trusted—a mother and pastor, but I determined to face the truth head-on. Before this nightmare, I had always tried hard to maintain integrity with my children. I knew that now their love would demand truth.

After I finished trying to explain the situation, I said, "Nicole and Rem, I need your forgiveness. I have sinned and I know it affects you deeply."

Nicole was quick to sit beside me and hold me close. "Mom, I do forgive you. I am proud of your courage in telling the truth. I will always be here for you. I love you so much."

Rem said, "Actually, Beth, I can see how you got trapped in this. I know the pain and desperation you were experiencing when you went to Bill for counseling in the first place. I know how vulnerable you were. You needed a safe place. I am really angry and disappointed with Bill. I've been meeting in a covenant group with him and three other guys with the intent to be honest and share our struggles. I have openly revealed those areas in my life. He's never hinted that there was anything wrong in his life. I feel betrayed by him."

Nicole continued, "To tell you the truth, I'm actually relieved. I knew something was desperately wrong when you called tonight. I thought you came to tell us you had attempted suicide. I've been so worried about you for so long. Mom, we're going to get through this together."

I called Zan and Amber in San Diego that evening. They, too, would hear the news only from me. Their reactions were very similar to Nicole and Rem's. "We love you and stand behind you. We're disappointed in Bill and how he has dealt with this whole situation. He should have been professional as a spiritual leader and counselor, but he took advantage of you when you were weak."

It was difficult to tell the truth to any of my children, but it was extremely hard to explain to Jessica. Even though for months I had tried to wear a mask before her which hid the true hopelessness I felt, I knew she was aware of my melancholy. It was time to help her understand.

I sat on the bed, and she lay beside me, and I told her of my obsessions for the first time. I started with the traumas of my childhood—death of my mother, abuses of my father and stepmother, and then nonspecifically explained that I had suffered with obsessive fears since I was twelve years of age. I told her it was because of this suffering that I went to Bill for help. I tried to be wise when I explained how I became entangled in an inappropriate relationship with him.

Jessica reached for me, put her head in my lap, and cried. "I love you, Mom. I'm sorry all this happened."

"I'm sorry, too, Jessica. I really am. I ask your forgiveness."

"I do forgive you, Mom."

At the time, she did not realize how she would be so devastated by the effects.

⊙〰〰◎

The next Sunday I did not sing in the choir. It was all I could do to get myself inside the door of the church. I waited until the service had already begun and then sat down in a back pew, hoping no one would notice me. Sean played the piano and then slipped in beside me.

As I watched Bill, I could tell from his pale, stoic countenance that he was severely distressed. The music was over and he walked up to the podium. He then introduced a professor from Denver Seminary who would be the special speaker that morning. As soon as he completed the formality, he walked off the platform, headed down the aisle through the congregation. He kept his head down and looked neither to the left or right before he slipped out the exit. I knew he was not only distressed: he was desperate!

I cried all afternoon. "Sean, I'm afraid Bill might commit suicide. I saw despair in his eyes today in church. The fact that he just walked out of the service lets me know it is serious. He has hinted to me that there were times when he has thought of taking his life. I would never forgive myself if he were to do that! And Pat wasn't there. That makes me wonder what's going on at their house."

⊙〰〰◎

Since neither Sean nor I had school on Monday of that coming week, we planned a Sunday night get-a-way. The Sheraton Hotel was not far from home, but it would give us an opportunity to be alone and try temporarily to shut out the crazy nightmare that was encompassing us.

The bright decor of our suite on the thirteenth floor provided an ambience of luxury and pleasure, but I struggled to be captured by its invitation. My terrorizing obsessions were a backdrop of darkness to everything I did or thought.

I tried to reassure myself, *"The world out there is totally crazy right now, but Sean and I have each other. I'm so thankful for that. So, I should be happy."* But, I found no peace.

As Sean and I tried to deal with the crisis, I vacillated between sadness, fear, panic, anger, and thanksgiving. I felt sadness and grief because I had lost Bill. I was fearful that he might choose to take his life. I was angry he had ever come into my life. I did not know how I was going to get through the trauma because now my tormenting obsessive thoughts had returned in a magnified measure.

I was thankful that I still had Sean's love and support. I cried until it seemed there were no more tears. Then I fell asleep in Sean's arms, only to wake up and cry some more. It was such deep pain, but somehow my tears cleansed deep within.

We talked, cried, loved, and held each other throughout the afternoon. As evening came, the room grew dark. We did not bother to turn on a light for somehow the darkness offered an escape. A place to hide. In the stillness, Sean said, "Beth, I love you very much. I want you to try to understand something. It seems overwhelming now, but we're going to get through this. Bill has his own choices to make, and whatever he chooses is his responsibility. Not yours. Do you understand that?"

"I'm trying," I said. "I'm really trying, but how am I going to get rid of these terrorizing thoughts? I've lost my counselor."

"We're going to find you a real one, Beth—one who can help you work through your fears, and one who can help you get through the mess Bill has created. There is a safe place out there, and we'll find it."

Sean's words were soothing. I inhaled a breath of relief for the first time in days. I did not realize it then, but Sean was helping me work through the early stages of debriefing. I had been brainwashed and did not know it. We held each other as we fell asleep.

⚬⚬⚬

We were startled from our sleep by the loud, intruding, hotel telephone above our heads. It took a few rings for us to process where we were and that it was the telephone. The darkness was eerie. Sean fumbled to pick up the receiver. I looked at the clock across the room. It read "11:30 p.m."

"Hello," he said..."You want to come and meet us here? Well, Sam, I don't know...."

I was fully awake by now, and my heart began to pound rapidly.

"I'll check with Beth." I heard the anxiety in Sean's voice. "Yeah, maybe it would be better if we came there."

As Sean hung up the receiver, I was wild with fear. I asked, "What did Sam want?"

Sean said, "He said he has something very urgent to talk to us about Bill. He wants to meet with us tonight. He and Edie were going to come here, but decided it would be better if we met them there since their kids are in bed."

"Sean," I cried, "I know Bill has done something stupid. It's what I was afraid of today. I'm afraid he has tried to take his life."

In the car driving toward the Landens' home, I shivered from horror. My heart felt like it was going to explode within my chest.

Sean said, "If he has done something extreme, Beth, remember it was his choice. He is not your responsibility."

"I just wish this was not happening. I wish this night were over."

◇▱▱◇

When Sam Landen answered the door, he did not seem too distressed. My heartrate began to slow. He ushered us into the family room where Edie sat at the table holding a cup of coffee. She was cordial in her greeting.

Sam said, "There is a matter we need to discuss. Would you guys care for some coffee, tea, or soda?"

"First," I said, "are Bill and Pat okay? I mean, well, I've been worried that he may have done something…"

Sam knew what I was trying to say. He gave a sympathetic smile when he answered, "Well, he has done some stupid things, but if you mean like trying to kill himself, no. However, he is stressed by this crisis!"

Edie prepared a pot of coffee as we took our seats at the dining table. As I sunk into the cushioned chair my shoulders drooped with relief. *Bill is still alive!*

After Sam apologized for calling us out of our place of retreat, he got to the point. "Pat is going to leave Bill."

"Oh no," I said. I was shocked, but at the same time not surprised. Pat told me on different occasions that unless things greatly improved in their marriage in one year, she was going to leave Bill. Whenever she would say that, I did not know if she was serious or joking.

Sean said, "What's he going to do?"

"Well," he said, "that's why I've called you here. I know that's going to impact things at the church, and I felt you should know about this first."

"I appreciate your telling us, Sam." Sean said. "What do you think Bill will do now?"

"I don't really know." he said.

90

"It's not good news that they are separating," Sean said, "but we'll have to admit, Beth and I are relieved it wasn't what we thought."

I said, "I want you and Edie to know I'm sorry that this whole ordeal has happened. I wish I could change it."

Sam said, "Beth, their separation is not really your fault. Pat has not been happy, and this was just the last straw."

When we finished our coffee, Sean said, "Well, Beth, we'd better get back to the hotel."

Sam said, "Again, I'm sorry to disturb you guys, but we figured you should find out first. Of course, this matter will have to come before the board and then the congregation, so you have a right to know first."

<hr />

It was early in the morning. Sean had just left for school and I was putting on the finishing touches of my makeup before walking out the door. The telephone rang.

"Hi, Beth. I think this is it," Ashley said. "My pains have been irregular since early this morning, but for the past few contractions, they've been every five minutes. They're definitely getting stronger."

"I'll be right there!" I anticipated this call, but now that it had finally approached, I felt unnerved. *God, help me to be strong for Ashley.*

I wasted no time in calling my school. "Hi, Lucy, I will not be coming in today. Ashley's in labor! Please get me a sub."

While driving to Ashley's, my thoughts went back seven months when Ashley came to tell Sean and me her husband had walked out on her. In fact, he went to New York and did not plan to come back. We knew they had experienced a stormy relationship, even before they were married, but we were shocked he had left her, particularly at this time. Ashley was two months pregnant. Even though she possessed a tenacious spirit of survival, she was devastated, feeling alone and vulnerable.

Thank God, Ashley Purdue had some advantages. Because she had worked hard to prepare herself professionally, was a successful teacher, and had strong support from her friends, she determined she was going to overcome. I admired her courage when she resolved to see that her baby receive all the love and nurturing she could give. Because she was like family, Sean and I pledged to walk beside her and help in any way possible.

I was honored when she asked me to coach her through childbirth. We attended all of the La Maze classes, practiced our breathing, and did our homework as we prepared ourselves physically and mentally for the anticipated event.

I could not believe she was ready to deliver. I was excited to be there for Ashley, and also to be there to hold her baby.

⚭

My exuberance was interrupted by a thought. *Edie Landen will be her nurse.* "*God, it's going to be so awkward, knowing she's in close contact with Bill. Ashley doesn't know the truth yet. Please don't let Ashley sense any tension. I don't want anything to take away from the reason I'm with her today—to help her deliver her baby safely.*"

The comfort of Edie's competent and familiar presence outweighed any apprehensions I felt during Ashley's labor.

My thoughts focused only on the needs of Ashley, a new mother struggling to give life to her baby. As contractions increased in intensity, our synchronized inhales and exhales gave way to pants. Then, one last push and Ashley's baby, Charity Purdue, was born.

The doctor said, "Ashley, your daughter looks healthy and beautiful." He looked at me, "Well, Coach, how would you like to cut the umbilical cord?"

"I would be honored."

⚬〰〰⚬

The following Sunday, the tinny words in Bill's brief sermon echoed their hollowness. He closed his Bible and picked up a paper from which he read, "Pat and I are having difficulty. She has left. We are separated." The congregation was stunned as he continued his announcement.

After the benediction, Bill took his usual place in the foyer where he shook hands and greeted people as they passed by. I stood at a distance, observing sad and disillusioned people crying. They gave Bill hugs and condolences as they passed him. It seemed like a funeral, and I felt the death was all my fault.

When almost everyone had gone, I stood next to Sean in the background. I wished there was something I could do or say to fix the situation, to turn the calendar back and make everything right. I wanted to go to Bill and tell him how sorry I was for what I had caused. I said to Sean, "Would you mind, or would it be inappropriate, if I said something to Bill?"

He seemed to understand my motives. "Go ahead, Beth. If you need to say something to him, go ahead."

I walked over to Bill. I was not sure exactly how to approach him. His arms hung limply at his side. He looked pale and drained. Cold. Blank.

I simply looked him in the eye and said, "I'm so..." my voice broke, "sorry, Bill." I braced myself to keep from crumbling into a pile of sobs.

With no expression, he spoke sternly, "Pat is really mad because you told Wanda what happened."

93

Wanda Landen had been a co-worker at church for months, and through that closeness, she and I had become friends. She, too, had experienced heartache. We had much in common, so I believed she could be a source of help in the midst of the trauma. After the news had gone public, I chose Wanda as the one person in which to confide my grief.

After I talked to Wanda, I realized it was not fair to put her in such a position. First, she was Sam's mother. She was also deeply committed to helping Pat and Bill. I did not know it, but the day I told her the news, Wanda had already set up a meeting to try to help Pat. The next day, at their meeting, Pat found out I, too, had talked to Wanda.

It only added more proof that the sick, entangled relationships had become crazy. It became another clue to me that Grace Church was not a safe place.

I said no more to Bill. I froze, turned, and walked away. When I got to the parking lot, Rem and Nicole wrapped me in their arms and ushered me into their car. "Get in, Beth," Rem said, "We're taking you home."

⚬⟱⟱⟱⚬

While Seth literally climbed into the toy box to look for his fire engine, Sean, Rem, Nicole, Jessica, and I sat together in the living room while each, in our own way, tried to talk through our grief. Sean said very little; he seemed lost in his thoughts. Rem played the role of facilitator as each of us tried to verbalize our feelings. Nicole and I spoke through our sobs. Jessica looked on as though she was not sure what was happening to her world. Seth was oblivious to any problems, as he continued to bury himself in the toy chest upheaval.

"I just don't understand," I said, "why I had such a strong reaction when I talked to Bill today."

Sean, Nicole, and Rem patiently listened as I tried to sort through it all. Their ideas and insights helped me to express my feelings.

I said, "I'll never go back to that church. I think what's happened today is I've received the final rejection from Bill, the rejection I've dreaded all along. I said 'goodbye' to him this afternoon. He's dead, as far as I'm concerned." Then anger flared, "He'll never do to me again what he did to me today and has done for the past few years! He will never mess with my mind again. I will tell anything I want, to anyone I want, whenever I want!"

Throughout the week, I experienced a certain amount of peace after the painful event with Bill that Sunday afternoon. I had entered the process of coming to grips with the truth. I indeed had said "goodbye" to Bill, and I would never again set myself up for his mind manipulation. With that small measure of understanding, I grasped hold of hope. I determined I would seek help to find my healing.

I never again set foot in Grace Church.

CHAPTER 9

THE SCHEME

Thursday afternoon the telephone rang. Sean answered. "Hello..."

I could instantly tell from the tone of his voice that he was talking to Bill. Fear erupted once again.

"I don't know. I'll have to discuss that with Beth."

His abruptness in hanging up the receiver revealed his confusion. He looked at me. "Beth, this is crazy. He wants to meet with both of us in his office this afternoon."

"No way! I protested. "I will not let him do it to me again. Whatever it is, I will not go. If you want to go, that's up to you. I will not be there. I cannot go!"

Sean said, "I don't know what he's up to. I'm going to go and find out."

"You don't have to, Sean. You can tell him there is no way you're going."

"I know that," Sean said confidently. "How about if I go and scout the situation? You stay here, and I'll go and see what this is all about. If I feel it is safe or necessary for you to be there, I'll call you. Will that be okay?"

"Okay. I'm so sorry you have to go through this mess, Sean."

"I'll be okay, Beth," he said as he kissed me on the forehead. "Please pray for me while I'm gone."

While he was gone, I did pray, as I kept waiting for the telephone to ring. *"What is this all about? Why would he want to talk to us? To me? God, please don't let the phone ring!"*

It was not long after that when the front door opened and Sean flung open the door yelling, "I can't believe what that man is trying to put over! The master manipulator is at it again!"

"What's going on, Sean?"

"I can't believe it, Beth! Listen to his scheme. 'Now that Pat is divorcing me, she is no longer in the way of my staying on as pastor. She never liked me in the ministry. So, now that she'll no longer be in the picture, I'm going to ask the church to forgive me, and then I'll withdraw my resignation. I want to stay on at Grace, and I want you and Beth to support me in that. I'm really sorry that Beth isn't here with you.' Can you believe him, Beth? He is sick!"

"What did you tell him?

Sean continued, "I told him if he did that, he was crazy. He would blow the church apart. He has gone before the congregation several Sundays in a row, each time changing his story. People are wondering what in the world is going on. What is the truth? The wheels are in full motion now for his resignation. If he goes through with this wild scheme, he'll divide the church. Some people were just looking for an excuse for him to leave, anyway."

I asked, "How does he plan to pull this off?"

"He wants to go before the congregation and tell them 'the truth' and then ask their forgiveness, so he may be reinstated," Sean said.

"So now it is going public!" I lashed. "Is he going to tell them who he was involved with? How selfish he is at everyone else's expense. This forgiveness idea is only to benefit him. He is not sorry. No, I change that. He's sorry alright, sorry he got caught!"

Sean said, "If he goes through with this demented plan, it will be the biggest mistake he has made yet."

The next afternoon Sean called from school to let me know he was going to stop by Bill's office to talk to him. "Beth, I told Bill in the beginning that I wouldn't accept the responsibility of making the decision for him concerning his resignation. The more I've pondered and stewed about it, the more I realize that I have to tell him that I feel he must resign. He's going to ruin the church if he goes through with this collusion. I'll be a little late, because I'm going to go talk to him before I come home."

Sean was not late coming home. He walked through the door right on time with a dejected look on his face. Joe Stoneman, the church chairman, had arrived before Sean to see Bill. "It's too late, Beth. I went by the church and saw Joe's car in the parking lot. That means he is hearing Bill's plan now. There's no way Joe will come out without buying into Bill's scheme. When he gets through with Joe…It's too late, Beth."

"How do you know, Sean?" I said. "Surely Joe will see through it. He'll want to hear my side of what happened. He will consider our family in this matter, won't he?"

"I'll be surprised if he doesn't buy into Bill's plan," Sean said. "Remember, Beth, how Bill uses his words to smooth things."

Sean kept going to the church throughout the afternoon to see if Joe had left. He needed an audience with Joe as soon as possible. However, Joe was there into the evening. The longer he was there, the more convinced we became that Bill was swaying him toward the idea that the resignation should be put aside and Bill stay on as pastor.

Even though Joe seemed to be somewhat loyal to Bill, he had always seemed to have high respect for our family—especially Sean. His wife Martha was one of my favorite people. I respected Martha's walk with God and always considered her someone to trust. She was real.

At 8:30 p.m., Sean checked the church again. "Joe is still with Bill. I wonder what's going on. I don't trust Bill. I have a feeling he is scheming a plan and is distorting the truth. I've got to talk to Joe tonight!"

⚬⟊⟊⟒

Sean was finally able to make contact with Joe at 9:00 that evening, but realized that he was indeed too late. Joe had bought into Bill's scheme; the church should forgive and allow Bill to keep his pastoral position. Joe did not ask the questions, "How are you, Sean? How is Beth? What really happened? How is your family?" He did reprimand, "You are angry, Sean. Why don't you just forgive Bill?"

Sean warned him, "Joe, if you go through with this crazy plan, I really believe it will cause a split in the church. One third of the people will leave."

But Joe could not see it, and he said, "I think you and the church need to forgive Bill."

⚬⟊⟊⟒

That became the motto of the friends of Bill in the arena of dissension in Grace Church. "If you forgive Bill, you will let him stay." It did not seem to matter that my family and I had been victimized, that we were bleeding to death. The Board of Elders did not ask me what had happened before they jumped into their campaign of "forgive and forget."

However, one major purpose was served when Bill pushed his schemes to stay. My loyalty turned from him. I was able to start the process of emotionally detaching myself from him. I began to understand that I truly had been abused by my pastor, Bill Morgan.

CHAPTER 10

A REAL COUNSELOR

I did not know where to turn to find a counselor, but I knew I could not go on without trustworthy professional help. The crazy, tormenting thoughts were in my mind day and night. They were the constant backdrop to the crisis that seemed so unbearable. I not only felt mortally wounded, but I carried guilt for hurting so many people—Sean, our family, Bill, his family, and the whole congregation. I also believed there would be effects that would ripple into the entire community. Because I taught in the local school, I worried that my students, their parents, and fellow staff members would somehow be damaged because of my sin. I had to have help!

My mind kept playing Bill's tapes, "All counselors are jerks...and if you ever do go to one, I only ask that you never go to Hal."

Hal Schmidt, a member of the congregation, was a marriage and family counselor. He often spoke in our church, and I always respected his genuine ability to communicate compassionately with those who suffered. Sometimes I pictured myself going to him with the dilemma in which I found myself with Bill, but I would quickly erase the idea because I had promised Bill that if I ever sought counseling elsewhere, it would not be Hal. So, I broke another promise to Bill when I made an appointment with Hal.

I knew Hal's heart ached as he listened to me unfold my traumatic story. It was not just for me, but for him and his church also. Hal's style was non-directive; he was not an advice giver. He was a caring listener who patiently allowed me to sort through my feelings during the great crisis. When I told him of my plan to leave Grace Church, he confirmed my decision when he said, "You are wise to remove yourself from the situation. The issue should not be, 'Is the church going to decide between keeping Bill or Beth?' The issue for the church is, 'Are they going to keep Bill?' Don't put yourself in the middle. They need to decide if he is worthy of the job." Hal was truly professional and trustworthy as he walked beside me through the darkness.

That evening my decision was further confirmed when I received a phone call from Edie Landen. I immediately perceived that the intent of her call was to drum up support for Bill. "Beth," she said, "you should be able to forgive Bill. Put all this in the past. Why can't you just come back and work with Bill? After all, you have your family. Bill has nothing." She may have meant well, but she had no idea what I was feeling, how deep were the wounds.

I saw myself as someone who had been repeatedly stabbed and was dying. It did not seem like the appropriate time to talk about forgiving the offender. I felt like one who was waiting for the arrival of an ambulance. I needed a tourniquet. I was bleeding to death.

That night I went to bed and cried myself to sleep. Sean came home from a board meeting at the church.

When he crawled into bed and snuggled next to me, I stirred.

Sean said softly, "Beth, are you awake?"

"Yeah."

He continued, "Sam Landen told me tonight that he thinks the church needs to forgive Bill and let him stay."

"That was the same phone conversation I had from Edie tonight. It seems like there's a collusion. I'm going to leave the church and get away from this mess! I've decided that I'm resigning my position as Director of Missions tomorrow. The church leadership is sick, and I've got to run for my life."

⊙〰〰〰⊙

As I awoke the next morning, a dramatic scene played across the screen in my mind. I had no doubt that God was giving me a definite directive, "Get Away!" The setting of the scene was several years previously, in the camp of the Jim Jones' Cult. My vision, however, deviated from the factual account of that event. I saw desperate people in total terror running through the woods, then tunneling underground, trying to make an escape. They successfully made it through to the other side of the forest, barely hanging onto their lives, when they saw a mass of people surround them. The escaping prisoners ran to them, expecting a rescue force to snatch them and carry them to safety. Instead, the expressionless people just stood there with their arms uniformly folded. They yelled, "No, you need to go back! Go back! He is your leader, and you need to work with him. It will be okay."

That scene faded into another. This time I saw myself. I was one of the people trying to escape. I felt as though I had been caught in some kind of "personal cult" with Bill. I felt brainwashed and desperately wanted to find freedom.

I was weak and afraid. I, too, mustered all the strength I could get, then started to tunnel my way out of the underground darkness. I pictured my forefinger scratching the dirt from within the suffocating hole. As my adrenalin took over, my forefinger gave way to both hands. They wildly clawed the dirt away until I burrowed my way under the wooded forest, until I thought I had arrived at a place where I was safe. I worked my way up through the dirt mound that encircled me. Then, I saw a speck of light, but because I had been in darkness so long, the sunlight blinded my eyes. I worked to adjust my focus, then continued digging until I was out. Free! I saw images. Familiar faces. My friends!

My legs wobbled, like a newborn calf learning to walk, but I gained strength as I struggled to my feet and began to put one lanky foot before the other. As my pace became coordinated, my gait turned to running. I began to laugh with relief. "I am going to be rescued! These people are my friends and they are going to help me!" I wildly flailed toward them, watching for their arms to reach out to snatch me to safety. But, I saw their stoic, blank-faced countenances and their folded arms. I knew something was wrong. In unison, they yelled, "Beth, go back! You must go back to him! Forgive him. Work with him. You will be okay."

I could hear Sean breathing next to me as I returned from my vision. He stirred, so I knew he was also awake. My heart pounded as I tried to unfold to him my early morning revelation. "Sean, I must get away from these people. It's dangerous here."

Sean said, "I agree, Beth. I'm going to try to stay on at the church until after the Christmas program. I'd like to conduct the choir in this last performance. I feel responsible to stay with it, if possible."

"I understand." I said. "Since you're leading it, you need to see it through. You must do what you need to do."

He continued, "If it gets too insane, I may have to resign before the program."

"What will happen to the program if you do leave?" I asked.

"At that point, it'll have to be their problem," he said.

CRULS

Within a few days, things did get crazier. The whole scene turned into a full-blown nightmare. Pat and Bill separated. Divorce proceedings were set in motion. The church's grapevine buzzed with information. The big debate, "Should Bill Morgan stay?", went into full swing as people took sides.

One camp said, "Our church needs to be a beacon of forgiveness. We need to forgive and forget. Forgiveness of Bill, and allowing him to be restored to his position as pastor, go hand-in-hand." Another group said, "Yes, we must forgive Bill, but that does not mean we should put him back into his place of leadership. He needs to resign and leave so that he can properly deal with the issues in his life. Forgiveness has nothing to do with him being reinstated as pastor." The third group simply said, "I am confused!"

CRULS

The day before the Christmas program there was another meeting of the church elders, where Bill presented his story of what had happened. I protested to the chairman. "The board hasn't bothered to contact me to hear my story!" It was at that point that they invited me to be present with Bill so that I could give my side of the story. I chose not to go, since I vowed I would never subject myself to his influence again. I also knew the cards were stacked against me.

Sean went to the meeting. He believed that his presence there would help honesty to prevail. It was not long into the meeting that he realized Bill was being encouraged to stay.

At that point Sean reached in his notebook and took out his resignation. He handed the letter to Joe Stoneman and said, "My family and I have served at this church for seventeen years. Our children have grown up here. This has been our church family, but we will not be able to stay at this church any longer. We need another shepherd. We need a place where we are safe. I don't know what you will do about the program tomorrow, but that will not be my problem." He presented them another sheet of paper. "Here is the outlined schedule for the Christmas Program. You can follow it if you like." Sean dropped the paper on the table, turned, and walked out of the meeting.

CHAPTER 11

A NEW CHURCH

The Sunday before Sean resigned, I visited South County Church. Jessica had attended some of the youth functions on occasions and enjoyed them. When it was necessary for me to find another church, that church came to my mind.

It was a large church, a mega church. I slipped in unnoticed and sat near the back. I looked around to see all the new faces. Since all my life I had attended small churches, it felt strange to be in such a huge crowd and not know a soul. Even though I felt lonely, I liked the anonymity. It felt safe.

I was drawn to the simplicity of the service. The music was contemporary and alive. The sermon was dynamic and clearly stated truths that I needed to hear, about myself and my relationship to God. I knew I had found the place where God wanted me. At the end of the service, as people lined up to shake hands with the pastor, I went out of my way to avoid having any contact with him. A pastor was the last person I wanted to greet. I slipped out the side door.

During the following week, Bill decided to leave Grace Church. Realizing the turmoil he had created with his decision to retain his position as pastor, he announced to the leadership that he was resubmitting his resignation so he could complete his doctoral program in counseling.

When the next Sunday rolled around, Sean joined me. His reaction to the new Church confirmed what I believed when he said, "This is the place where we can work through the process of healing. This will be a safe place."

⚬══════⚬

My obsessive thought patterns became more and more unmanageable. I had to deal with the injuries of the crisis, but even more urgent was the need to find relief from uncontrollable thoughts. I was convinced I was going crazy. I wanted a professional, someone with expertise in counseling people with obsessive-compulsive symptoms such as mine, to say, "This is what is wrong with you. You are not the only person with this problem. You would never act out your aggressive thoughts. You are not crazy, and here is how we're going to deal with it."

It was at this point that I decided to find that particular counselor. Hal Schmidt had been such a help in aiding me in the urgency of my trauma, and he probably would have guided me to the place where I would have been able to work through the symptoms of my illness, but I was impatient. My despair drove me to seek an immediate, tangible solution.

Sean and I decided that, in my search for therapy, I should start at the Counseling Center at South County Church. They had a large staff of trained personnel, including full-time therapists as well as interns.

When I made my phone call, I said, "I want an

appointment with the person who has the most experience."

"Well," the receptionist said, "that would be Dr. Samuel Jensen. He is the director of the Center."

"Is it possible to get an appointment with him?" I asked, thinking that since he was in the top position, my chances would be slim."

"Let me give you his phone number. He has his own private practice, and you can call him there," she said.

I hung up the receiver and redialed. After the phone rang two times, he answered, "This is Dr. Jensen. May I help you?"

I could tell by his soft voice that he was an older man. *Oh, good! He's been around for awhile. He probably has had experience with cases such as mine.*

"Yes," I said, "my name is Beth Van Dyke, and I'm interested in an appointment. I called the Center and they referred me to you. Do you have any available time?"

"Yes," he said, "I could see you this Thursday at 4:00."

On Monday evening I had my last appointment with Hal. It was with the highest respect for him that I expressed my gratitude for what he had done on my behalf. "I have made an appointment with Dr. Samuel Jensen at South County Counseling Center."

He smiled, "Oh, Dr. Samuel Jensen has been around for awhile. In fact, he has written psychology textbooks, and I've read some of them."

I thought, *Oh, relief. I'm on the right track. If he has written textbooks, then surely he'll know what's wrong with me!*

Dr. Jensen's office was a pleasant suite on the third floor of a medical building in northern Denver. I could see the magnificent Rockies through the large office window. The views of splendor did not take away my doubts. *Am I ever going to get help? God, how long is it going to take to find answers and healing? Please let Dr. Jensen know what to do!*

I was not prepared for my initial introduction of the distinguished looking Dr. Samuel Jensen, when he came to greet me in the waiting room. His silver gray hair, slow gait, short awkward steps, and soft rasping voice revealed that he truly was an older man. *Oh dear, he might die on me before I can get through this!* I continued to talk to myself as I followed him into his office. *It's going to be okay, Beth. You wanted someone with experience. He wouldn't be practicing if he wasn't up to it. Besides, you don't have to worry about romantically attaching yourself to him. He could be your grandfather. This will be a safe place.*

☙〰❧

I trusted myself into the care of Dr. Jensen for the next four months, as he worked diligently to help me try to overcome my obsessive thoughts, which seemed to be growing in severity.

"What is wrong with me, Dr. Jensen?" I pleaded one day.

He smiled when he answered, "Beth, you are a very creative person. You are like a colorful, delicate butterfly fluttering around from one obsession to another."

I was amused by his reply, but chuckles soon turned to tears. "Why do I do it? So much of my energy goes into coming up with something else to obsess on. It's like I sabotage myself over and over, and I can't stop! I'm going crazy! What's wrong with me?"

He reassuredly said, "Beth, there is a common thread running through all this, and we will find it."

I contemplated his words and then pleaded, "Please help me, Dr. Jensen. Help me find that thread!"

After the telephone rang two times, I picked up the receiver. "Hello, Beth Van Dyke? This is Mrs. Jensen. We will need to cancel your appointment with Dr. Jensen tomorrow. He's in the hospital for some tests. He's not feeling well. He'll try to see you next week."

A week later he was still in the hospital. Dr. Samuel Jensen tried to continue his practice, but his health would not permit it. He called me one day to give me the news. "I'm going to have to refer my patients elsewhere because of my health. I'm not sure exactly what's wrong, but it may take some time to get back on my feet."

"I'm sorry to hear that you're not well," I selfishly thought.

"I have a recommendation for another therapist for you," he said. Her name is Ann Paxton. She's at the church's Counseling Center."

"But," I doubted, "do you think she can handle my case?"

"I think she will be perfect for you. She's the best!" he said. "She will be calling soon to set up an appointment."

CHAPTER 12

ANN PAXTON

From the beginning, my therapist-client relationship with Ann Paxton was tailor-made. Her warm confidence glowed as she made her introduction. We were about the same age; yet, I felt like a child in her presence. Ann symbolized the parent I had lost as a child. It was at that point my journey with Ann began.

Ann pulled a wand from her shelf. "See this wand. It is to remind you that I have no magic. It takes work, hard work, to get to wholeness and healing. But, I have a strong faith that God does heal, and I pray that for all my clients. I believe Jesus will walk with us through each step of the process."

Feeling secure in that knowledge, I sketched my story to Ann, starting with my childhood traumas and continuing on into the events that included my painful involvement with Bill. While I told my story, I interwove how, starting at age twelve, the obsessive fears began to plague me. Then, with Ann's gentle probing, she challenged me to go back and stir painful scenes stored in my memory.

Ann was an active and compassionate listener. There

were tears in her eyes as I relived the painful events of my past. She said, "We're going to go back and help you find healing from those memories, Beth. Jesus and I will walk with you."

I struggled on my quest to receive healing from all the painful experiences, losing my mother as a child, father's physical, sexual, and emotional abuse, stepmother's hate, pastoral abuse, and finally church's abuse. Always in the forefront was the burning question, "Why do I torture myself with the terrorizing thoughts?" Whenever I got discouraged, Ann would say, "Keep working, Beth. We are going to find that thread Dr. Jensen talked about. You will discover how you can overcome these tormenting obsessions."

God led Ann Paxton and me step-by-step down each dark corridor, each hidden room, and as we went, we brought light to every secret chamber of my past. As we shined the beam of light on all the haunting secrets, the binding chains were loosed. As our searchlights exposed the lies; they were replaced with truth.

Then Ann became the object of my attachment, and I became afraid. I found that I had some of the same emotions toward Ann I had towards Bill. *Something is wrong with me! Maybe my sexual orientation is twisted. Perhaps I'm*—I was afraid to think the word—*homosexual.* But Ann protected my vulnerability as she helped me work through the reality of what was happening. I saw truth. As I swept away the phantom of my fear of intimacy, I saw it for what it really was. I longed for parent-love. I then understood how my feelings toward Bill did not really stem from a sexual need. I had desperately yearned to fill the aching void deep, deep inside: my parent-loss.

As my therapy with Ann progressed through difficult issues, I again became like the creative butterfly. My obsessions flared. I started looking for ways to destroy the lifeline that Ann represented. *What can I say to shock her—to sabotage our relationship so that she will not be here for me? What if I drive her away? Then, I will have to get another therapist. Then, I will do the same to that person. I can have no therapist! There is no hope! I want to die!* On and on it went. Day and night. My thoughts were literally driving me crazy.

Ann was a hero. She tenaciously hung with me through all the stuff I handed her. At times I sensed Ann's frustration in knowing how to deal with all of my ruminations, but Ann would not give up.

One time I asked her, "Are you ready to give up on me?"

Ann said, "No, Beth. We're going to find an answer for you even though sometimes I'm not exactly sure how to help you manage your obsessions. You know, I read an article in a journal this week about obsessive-compulsive disorder. Of course, I thought of you. It stated that it's successfully being treated with medication. In fact, I have the article with me, and I want you to read it. Perhaps your family doctor can prescribe medicine. At least it's a possibility. God is looking out for you, Beth. I'm sure he directed me to the article."

I respected Ann's honesty when she admitted she was not exactly sure how to deal with my symptoms. By this time, I had full confidence in her integrity and had enough faith that God was going to direct us to a source of help.

Two weeks later I was in a session with Ann. Her eyes sparkled with excitement when she said, "Beth, I went to a seminar last weekend and heard a psychiatrist speak on the subject of 'obsessive-compulsive disorder.' It was so interesting. Dr. Loren Johnson, the doctor who spoke, has a practice in the area. I think it might be good if you make an appointment with him. If you do need medication, he can prescribe it. How would you feel about going to see him?"

"Can I still work with you if I go see him?" I asked.

"I'm sure we could work that out. I'm very interested to learn more about your condition. Do you mind if I call and confer with him?"

"Of course not," I said. "I've got to find relief."

⟨✦⟩

At the end of my first appointment with Dr. Johnson, I said, "Doctor, can you tell me what is wrong with me?"

He turned in his burgundy leather swivel chair to face me and simply said, "Yes, Beth, I can. You have obsessive-compulsive disorder. It is a physical condition. It is something you can not help. It is genetic; so someone in your family probably had it. The good news is we can treat it with medication…"

As he spoke, I grabbed hold of his words. They rang in my head. These obsessions stem from a physical condition! It's a physical condition! I can't help it! There is hope!

⟨✦⟩

I continued to see Ann Paxton for six months following my discovery of the basis of my lifelong mental disorder. She helped me find healing and bring closure to all the emotional issues that plagued my life. Being able to forgive—Bill Morgan, Grace Church, and others who had inflicted pain—was not an easy task. But it was necessary before I could get on with my life.

On May 5, 1989, with sadness, but with celebration, I had my last appointment with Ann Paxton. She was my faithful companion who walked with me on the long journey to find restoration and wholeness. In her, I learned that I could once again trust.

118

CHAPTER 13

RESPONSIBILITY

The day dawned when sunlit streams of restoration beamed rays of life into my soul. Strength surged through my veins and I no longer felt myself the helpless victim. Pain, anger, and fear no longer drove me to reactions. As I examined my motives, my concern focused on protecting other potential victims. I knew God wanted me to take responsible action.

It was during my months of therapy with Ann that I took steps to notify the Colorado Department of Consumer Affairs of my complaint against Bill Morgan. I communicated that I was sure he was counseling somewhere in a clinical setting.

The answer was that since he had not applied for his state license, there was nothing they could do at that point. "We will flag his name so that if he ever makes application for license, we'll follow up at that time. What you need to do now is to contact the supervisor wherever he is counseling."

I did not know who to contact. Then, one day I stumbled onto a seminary publication announcing that Bill had completed his doctorate with a degree in Counseling. There was his picture as big as life. He was proudly standing next to the chairman of the Psychology Department, holding his diploma.

I wasted no time in contacting the seminary, including a copy of the formal complaint I had sent to the state. Sean was shocked when within that week, he received a call at work from Bill, stating that he wanted an appointment with both of us. He wanted to "make amends."

My immediate reaction was, "No way will I talk to him. I said I would never again subject myself to his manipulation. I just can't do it!"

However, as I considered the thought of facing him and allowing him to express whatever he needed to say, I began to reconsider. I prayed, "God, help me to do the right thing." I knew if I was going to break the power he had over me, it would be in my best interest to go through with the meeting. I told Sean, "If we do talk to him, it will not be in his office where he can use his words and manner to intimidate. It will be in our home, on 'my turf.'"

Sean said, "I think you should call him yourself and set up the meeting. You be in charge, Beth."

I knew Sean was correct. I said, "God, give me courage to go through with this," as my shaky hands picked up the telephone and dialed his number. Confidence grew as I took initiative.

"Hello, Bill. This is Beth Van Dyke. I am calling in regard to your request to talk to me and Sean."

"Yes, I would like to do that whenever it is convenient for you," he said.

I said, "We can meet with you this Friday evening at 7:00 P.M.

He paused, then responded tentatively, "Okay."

I did not give him the opportunity to suggest we come to his office. "I would like for the meeting to be in our home."

"O—okay."

I gave him our address with directions and ended the conversation, "Sean and I will see you this Friday at 7:00 P.M."

I put the receiver down. *Jesus, I know I must do this. Please help me get through it.*

⌘

Friday evening the doorbell and the seventh chime on our grandfather clock rang simultaneously. Sean opened the door to greet Bill Morgan. I hesitated in the kitchen. *Thank you, Father, that I'm a changed person. Thank you for my husband Sean. Give him an extra measure of strength today.* I took a deep breath and walked to Sean's side. I reached out and shook Bill's hand and then motioned him into the living room to sit down. I took my seat in the armchair across from him. I felt calm confidence within.

After a few words of light exchange, Bill got to the point of his purpose for the meeting. "I'm very sorry for what happened. I was wrong." Bill clearly stated that he was responsible for allowing the inappropriate relationship between us.

I listened to each word trying to discern sincerity. I thought, *I only wish this apology had not been solicited. If I had not written the seminary, I'm sure he wouldn't be here now. He was backed into the wall. What else could he do? Yet, I want to believe him.*

Sean said, "Since you continue to counsel, I need to know what you've done to guarantee this type of thing will not happen again?"

Bill reassured, "I've received personal counsel as well as taken a seminary class on counseling ethics."

I said, "I have forgiven you, but I need to know that something like this will not happen again.

"It will not," he said. "I know I did a stupid thing. However, I am not a stupid person. I am very sorry."

When our conversation took a turn from apology and forgiveness to casual talk, I breathed relief. *I have done what I needed to do, God. Only you know Bill's heart and motives. I'm going to accept his apology as honest and sincere. If he's only sorry he got caught instead of truly sorry for his deeds, then you'll have to deal with him. I choose to forgive him.*

CHAPTER 14

SAFE CHURCH?

With exuberance, I stood singing with the congregation as the praise and worship band led, "Thy Word is a lamp unto my feet, and a light unto my path…" I remembered singing this same song the very first time I took my seat at South County Church. My life had been in such mental turmoil back then, but now my heart was light and my song was joyful. *God, I love you. I'm so thankful for this church. I remember how alone, fearful, and despairing I was the first Sunday I slipped into this auditorium, but, this is where I've found healing. Thank you for this church.*

The senior pastor got up to speak. His sober demeanor, and immediate lack of humor, signaled that something was wrong. He pulled a sheet of paper from his Bible. He spoke, "Today will not be an ordinary sermon. I would like to read what I have to say."

My heart sank. *What's he going to say? Please don't say anything weird—like you're resigning or…*

He said, "This church has always taught forgiveness. I want you to know that I, too, have feet of clay."

I felt weak. Nauseated. *Please don't let him say that he's been involved in sexual sin!*

"I have worked under a lot of stress." He continued. "I've needed to take time off. Being your senior pastor has brought responsibilities that seem overwhelming at times. During this, I found myself involved in an inappropriate relationship with a woman…"

I don't want to hear this! I don't want to hear this! I mentally put my hands over my ears trying to shut out his words.

"There was no sexual intercourse."

No! This message sounds like a tape recording of Bill Morgan. The script is the same. I can't take this. "Please, God, spare me from hearing this. I denied, *This is not happening!*

He continued to read his confession statement to the congregation. He ended with saying that he needed a leave of absence so that he could be renewed. His whole speech took less than five minutes.

As death's cold grip chokes out life, the pastor's shocking announcement stunned the congregation. The eerie silence seemed to reveal what I was feeling. Confusion. Disappointment. Disbelief.

My immediate thoughts circumvented the pastor. *What about her—the woman with whom he's been involved? What about her family? Does she have a husband? Does she have children? What's going to happen to this church? What about me? Who can I trust? Will I be able to continue here? I thought this was a safe place.*

Even though Sean and I had given so much of our lives to being active in church work, God knows how tempted we were to give up attending church at all as we struggled with cynicism. However, we decided that we would give our best effort to stay at South County

Church. There was no other church we could trust. So, we took a leap of faith, hung on for dear life, and left it up to God to take care of us.

∾⤳⤸

The pleasant aroma of Sean's freshly brewed morning coffee drew me downstairs. I proceeded to pour the cream into the dark brown liquid, watching it turn to a perfect rich tan. I knew it was going to be a good day.

At 10:00 the night before, we had just returned from our second trip to Europe, which ended in a tour of the East Coast. We had been gone for six weeks, and it felt good to be home. We sat at the dining room table, hastily sorting through the pile of mail which lay heaped on the table.

Our previous trip to Europe had been so stressful, as I struggled to deal with the entanglement with Bill. This trip was a satisfying contrast. Warm and vivid memories of loved ones and places we had visited were fresh in my heart and memory. I could picture riding bikes with Zan, Amber, and our two year old grandson Harrison in Berlin on the bike path that, only a few months before, had been the Berlin Wall. I could see and hear Harrison say, "Nan, let's go to the spielplatz. That would be fun!" I smiled. *God, thank you for allowing me such a special time this summer. Thanks for the freedom I experienced. I'll always cherish the memories.*

My cheerful thoughts were interrupted by the ring of the telephone. I lifted the receiver. "Oh, hi, Ashley…Our trip was great…Yeah, we'll be at home tonight. Ashley, are you okay? You just seem so anxious to talk to us…Sure, 7:00 is fine."

As soon as I put the receiver down, Sean said, "What's going on with Ashley?"

"I don't know. She sounded strange. I can sense when she's struggling. Something's not right, Sean. She'll be here tonight. She said she needs to talk to us."

∽𝕿𝕿𝕿𝕿𝕿∾

It was a merry atmosphere as Jessica, Sean, Nicole, Rem, their three boys, Sean, and I arrived at the restaurant for our "Welcome home" dinner party. I had my grandsons Seth, now age four, on one arm, and Brian, age two, on the other. Sean was carrying six-month-old Allen.

Rem held the door open as we entered. I said to Nicole, "Ashley called today. She sure sounded like something was wrong." As soon as I spoke the words, the expression in Nicole's eyes changed from merriment to concern. I knew she knew something I did not. I asked, "Is she in trouble?"

"Mom, Ashley has talked to me, but I'm not supposed to say anything. She wants to talk to you herself."

I blurted out the first thing that flashed through my mind, "Is she pregnant?"

"No, it's not like that."

"Well, what is it?" I pushed.

"She is dating someone."

"Who is it?"

"I can't tell. She'll tell you about it when she comes tonight."

"Why is it so mysterious?" I was really curious by now. "Is it someone I know?"

"Yes," Nicole said.

Thinking the worst I asked, "He's not married, is he?"

"No, but he has been. He's divorced now."

A name blazed through my mind and my gut cringed. I whispered, "Nicole, is it Bill? Bill Morgan?"

Her look told me I was right. Anxious energy sent shock waves through my body. I became numb and weak and had to sit down on the bench in the waiting section of the restaurant. I wanted to cry out. Panic started to overtake. *Beth, this isn't true. Ashley wouldn't do this.*

"Mom," Nicole's words penetrated, "she's been dating him since before you left for Europe. I've been dealing with it all summer." Tears filled her eyes. "It's been so hard. Yes, Mom, it's true. That's what she wants to tell you tonight."

As we sat on the sofa, Ashley, who had become like part of our family, proceeded to tell us about her relationship with her former pastor and counselor, Bill Morgan. "I've been dating Bill all summer." Tears filled her eyes, "I know it's crazy and I keep asking myself, 'What am I doing? How can it all work together?' But, I've come to care about him a lot."

"Bill Morgan." I cried, "Why him, Ashley?" I searched for something to say; but there was nothing to say. All I could do was cry. Finally, I said, "I don't know what I'll do. You're going to have to give me time to sort this out. But, regardless of what I decide, Ashley, I want you to know that I love you. Maybe I won't be able to go along with you on this one. Maybe I'll have to love you enough to release you."

"But what about the whole issue of forgiveness? Why can't you just forgive…"

Here it is again. Bill's tapes keep playing. Now, his words are coming through her. Can I ever get away from him?

Sean spoke, "Ashley, the banker may screw me over. I can forgive him, but that doesn't mean I'll ever trust him with my money again."

For days I wrestled with the anguish of a dilemma that seemed overwhelming. I felt raped by the invasions of circumstances beyond my control that brutally stirred incomprehensible emotions. Passions of fear, anger, love, hate, all wrapped up together, penetrated my soul.

Dark clouds of depression once again dropped their asphyxiating blankets. As before, bed became my recoil. I lay curled in a fetal ball, my body uncontrollably shaking. Tormenting tapes played in my head. *You shouldn't have told. It has destroyed everything. There will be no end to the effects of my sin. They'll go on forever.* I prayed, "God, I'm so sorry. I've messed up life for so many people. It's put a wedge between Nicole and Ashley, Jessica and Wendy. On and on it goes. I feel damned if I do and damned if I don't. I can't tell Ashley not to love Bill. But, I can't be part of his life either. I want to die. Please, God, take me home, out of this never-ending mess."

The following morning I awoke with a clear direction. I believe it was from God. "ENOUGH IS ENOUGH! You are no longer a victim, Beth. You need not subject yourself to Bill Morgan again. It may mean the pain of losing Ashley, but you must protect yourself. Only you and I know the depths of the pain this has caused. Only you can make the decision. Others may not understand, but you need only answer to Me."

"But God, I'm finding it so hard to forgive him."

God's presence enveloped me. I sensed Him saying, "I know, Beth, and where you feel inadequate to forgive, please give it to Me. That's where My grace will be sufficient. Just stay close to Me."

For the rest of the day and the days that followed, the words, *"Enough is enough,"* were imprinted in my mind.

I knew, as painful as it was going to be, that I had my answer. It was as though I was losing a daughter and a good friend. I felt robbed that I would be losing the bond with her child, Charity, who had become like a grand-daughter. It was a tough-love choice when I expressed to Ashley my decision, "If you travel this road, you'll have to travel this one without me." As much as I love them, as much as Ashley desired to fit it all together, I knew that it could not happen. On May 11, 1992, our thirty-second wedding anniversary, Ashley Purdue married Bill Morgan.

꩜

Our senior pastor at South County Church resigned and left his wife. A short time later he started a new church in the area. The assistant pastor who took over the position as senior pastor, also resigned in less than a year. Why? A few months later, it was public knowledge that he had committed adultery. Soon he started a church in our neighborhood. A third pastor on the staff at our church, resigned his position and left his wife—a dear friend of mine. The reason? Another woman involved…

CHAPTER 15

ANSWERS TO MY OWN QUESTIONS

In spite of my personal fight to overcome the injury caused by a pastor's violation of power, a congregation's inability to deal properly with the issue, and subsequently, three other pastors falling to immoral acts, the haunting question remains, *What About Her?* The conclusion of my story does not end with resolution—the cycle only continues. This is essentially the reason I chose to share my story. With a passion to see the abhorrent cycle stop, I conclude my book with three letters.

Dear Pastor,

Please understand this letter is prompted by some traumatic events involving my pastors in recent years. It has taken many months, even years, of therapy and soul-searching for me to be able to even want to address you. I can now approach you with cautious respect.

As a child growing up in the church, I had a deep lack of parental love and support. Consequently, I looked to my pastor as God's parent model. Thank God, I was fortunate to have pastors during those years of my life who were aware of my need to be protected and nurtured. It was their affirmation and acceptance that drew me to my Heavenly Father. For that I am eternally grateful.

When I was an adult facing a crisis, I sought counsel with my pastor. At the time, I was not conscious of the dynamics, but I still carried that need for parent love and approval. Consequently, I transferred that need to him. That is when I fell prey to a man who was as needy, if not more needy, than I.

It is with respect that I address these issues. I know you are human and experience the same temptations as those of us in your congregation. Because of the public nature of your job, many times you are overworked, open to unfair judgment, criticized, and misunderstood. However, you chose this profession. Hopefully, you feel God called you to the sacred trust.

My insights come from what I learned from my experience. As I journeyed through the painful healing process, I came to realize that my exploitation was a classic case. Therefore, I offer my exhortation:

(1) Know yourself. Of all the people in your congregation, you should lead in the search to intimately know yourself. Before you took the sacred position, you should have undergone a deep process of personal examination. Hopefully, some of that took place in your professional training. If not, you need to find the resources. You must continually do as David when he expressed, "Search me, O God, and know my heart: try me, and know my thoughts," Psalm 135:23. It is imperative that you know your vulnerabilities—your blind spots.

(2) Don't isolate yourself. One of the systemic clergy profile traits is a chronic lack of intimacy. Being the leader can be a lonely position; so it is important that you surround yourself with a network of men for the purpose of friendship, support, and accountability. It may be other pastors, but it must be a small group where you can be real.

(3) Remember, only Jesus is the Savior. You are not a grandiose caretaker. That notion is a pride setup. Don't allow people to put you on a pedestal. Their temptation to put you there will diminish if you stay humble. God simply asks you to be his servant leader—to guard the flock he has entrusted to you.

(4) Keep your role clear. Are you a pastoral leader or a therapist? When I sought help from Bill Morgan, I needed a skillfully trained therapist and medical doctor (psychiatrist). Of course, at the time, I was desperate and unaware of what I needed. From the onset, my pastor should have referred me to a professional who was qualified to deal with my complex problems.

Even if you are trained in clinical counseling, and you are pastor of a church, I believe you are taking an unwise risk to embark on therapy with a parishioner in your congregation. The code of ethics in the American Counseling Association highly discourages dual role relationships with a client. As pastor you take on multiple role connections, such as spiritual leader, friend, friend to the family, and staff member. All of these roles were involved between Bill Morgan and myself. When we embarked on therapist/client, another dynamic entered. Bill Morgan could not be objective. It was a setup for disaster.

(5) Guard yourself. I may come across as legalistic in this area, but you can't be too careful. If a woman in your congregation needs counseling which requires more than

spiritual guidance, refer her to a qualified professional. If it is spiritual counseling which requires more than one session, if possible, include her spouse. If she is single or it is impossible for her spouse to be there, include your wife or another staff member in the session. If that is impossible, keep the door ajar. For sure, have a window in your office door. Never lock the door! If you find yourself attracted to this person, let another staff member deal with her. DO WHATEVER YOU NEED TO DO to guard your integrity and the safety of the person seeking help.

Please, please, please, I need you to stay morally pure! My earnest prayers are with you,

Beth Van Dyke

○〜〜〜○

Dear Church,

You were there for me and my family the day I was born. I have never known life without you. It was in your nurturing that I found Jesus. I love you for that.

When I was a vulnerable eleven year old, it was people in the body of Christ who wrapped their tender arms around me at the time of my mother's death. When I suffered from physical and emotional neglect by my father, those same dear ones found creative ways to protect me. Your love was strong as God used your agents to keep the umbrella of protection over me. I love you for that.

It was other ministering arms in the body who saw to it that I got to college. There I found my Christian husband who has loved me unconditionally. At our Christian wedding, we committed our lives to making God the center of our home. Throughout the years, we actively served in various roles of service in our church.

God, so mercifully, gave us three wonderful children, whom we raised in the arms of the church. We dedicated each infant to God. We were committed to raising them to feel secure and nurtured as part of the church family. At young ages, they all discovered a personal relationship with Jesus Christ. As they grew into teenage years, they took on leadership roles in the church and school. There they became beacons of God's love to their peers. They all married Christian spouses. As they began having children, they dedicated each one of our grandchildren to God.

After I escaped the four year entanglement with Bill, the church betrayed our family. We cried out for help, but the leadership of our local church turned a deaf ear. They did not understand our anguish. They seemed upset that I had "told." Their compassion and support went to the pastor.

Church leaders, here is what I and the other "hers" need from you:

PREVENTION

(1) *Hold your pastor/pastors accountable.* They are called (or should be called) to protect and guard "the flock." Even though pastors are the primary leaders of the church, they are still human; therefore, they need a small strong support group where they are expected to be honest about their personal struggles.

(2) *Be discerning of their authenticity, or lack thereof.* Pastors' personal lives should equate with what is being preached from the pulpit. Of course, this does not mean they are perfect, but they do need to confess humbly their shortcomings. There should be an overall evidence of the spiritual fruits within their families. Sometimes the general laity can be deceived, so part of your responsibility is to keep authenticity in check.

WHEN AN ABUSE HAPPENS

(1) *Take strong leadership.* Abuse is any form of an authority figure taking advantage of any person that is vulnerable. It could be verbal violations, emotional exploitation, physical misuse, or blatant sexual abuse. In my case, the emotional and physical involvement was almost as intense, if not more so, than a full sexual relationship. When this occurs, the pastor must step down from leadership; and you, the leadership, need to take full control. You become the shepherd of the flock. All involved, including the church constituency, need to feel that security.

(2) *Go directly to the victim/victims.* Statistics show that when there has been an immoral sexual act against a parishioner, chances are there are other victims. Immediately go to the known victims. That includes the persons abused and their families. They are in a state of deepest injury and need prompt intervention. Listen thoroughly to them. They are in desperate crisis and need you to believe them. They need reassurance you are going to help them find help.

(3) *Provide them with counseling service.* If your church is large enough to provide a professional counseling staff, that may work if it is agreeable with the victims. Probably the best situation would be for them to get help from another place that can be objective and provide a comfortable atmosphere for the injured.

(4) *Get the pastor away from the local church.* When misconduct has happened, provide safety for the victims and others in the congregation by removing the perpetrator from the scene. This is not the time for the discussion, "Will we allow him to remain in a position of leadership, or can he remain as part of our local fellowship?" The pastor does need help, but this church is not the place. He

needs to be in a place where his problem can objectively be addressed.

Keeping him on-site will only cause divisions within the church body. He *must* leave so that he, the victims, and the church can find healing.

When the pastor has been involved in sexual abuse, he and the church are susceptible to legal suits. More and more, the problem is "coming out of the closet," and laws protect rights of the victims. More and more churches are being forced to deal with law suits.

(5) *Do not confuse forgiveness with restoration to leadership.* These are two separate issues. The pastor who has sexually and mentally abused members of his congregation, needs to step out of leadership, experience true repentance, find restoration with God, and then be reconciled with his family.

(6) *Victim healing is a process.* One of the deepest hurts for me, right after I disclosed the secret, was when members of the church called to inform me that I needed to forgive the pastor and put it all behind me. Of course, forgiveness is necessary, but this is not the time to approach that subject. They need time to process what has happened to them. Allow them time to go through the steps of recovery.

Victims usually do not even realize they have been violated. In fact, they believe it is all their fault. When I told my first therapist what happened, he said, "You sound just like an abused child." That truth jolted me into the reality. Help them to see that truth.

It was important for me to confess my sin to God so that I could experience his love and forgiveness. That gave me freedom to feel all the emotions which released me to eventually be healed. After I recognized I truly had been abused, I felt anger. It was a competent therapist, a loving husband, and supportive children who gave me permission to express that emotion. As they gave me permission to do so without judgment, I was able then to move into the process of forgiveness. Perhaps I could have arrived there sooner had the church allowed me to experience those feelings.

Please love and support the victims by giving them permission to be who they are as they process the trauma and seek recovery. Pray for them in love. If you are there to care for them, in God's time, *He* will help them forgive.

So, dear church, even though I've been tempted to give up on you, I have not done so. I desperately need you. I pray that you will be dynamic and healthy as you guard even the weakest in God's family. *"I tell you the truth, whatever you did for one of the least of these sisters and brothers of mine, you did for me,"* Matthew 25:40 NIV.

Love from your sister,

Beth Van Dyke

CRULD

Dear Victim,

In my story, I have tried to draw a vivid picture of all the dynamics involved in my relationship with Bill Morgan. It would be redundant to expound on that any further. However, there are some things I yet want to say to you.

Only God knows the circumstance in which you find yourself. You may be in the early temptation stage of venturing into an inappropriate relationship with your pastor. Perhaps you are ecstatic and enjoying an existing emotional and physical involvement. It could be you are in a place where your emotions shift from moment to moment and you're confused, loving it, yet feeling guilty and trapped. You may be desperately praying you could escape the deadly trap but see no way out. Maybe you are trying to put your life back together after ending sexual abuse by your pastor or counselor. I want you to know, regardless of where you are, God wants to rescue you and help you find healing.

You need to know:

(1) *You are not alone!* It is a sad fact, but sexual abuse by the clergy, of one degree or another, happens all too often. In the book BETRAYAL OF TRUST by Stanley Grenz and Roy D. Bell, they state, "The tragedy has reached epidemic proportions." Since my recovery, I have talked to women, attended seminars and conferences dealing with this issue, and have realized there are many "hers" out there.

(2) *It was not your fault!* A relationship involving sexual misconduct between a pastor and parishioner is not the same as an adult consensual sexual affair.

An article in **The Christian Century**, *"Blaming Women for the Sexually Abusive Male Pastor,"* written by Ann-Janine Morey, associate professor of religious studies at Southern Illinois University in Carbondale, Illinois, she quotes Marie Fortune, executive director of the Center for the Prevention of Sexual and Domestic Violence in Seattle. "A male pastor's sexual advances toward a woman that occur while he performs his professional duties are better understood as 'sexual abuse.' Whereas the term 'adultery' implies that both participants are consenting equals, the term 'sexual abuse' assumes that a person has used personal, social or physical power to coerce sexual intimacy."

In the same article, Ann-Janine Morey states, "Sexual abuse by pastors exhibits the same dynamic as incestuous

What About Her?

abuse, which takes place within the context of an intimate relationship (family, church, counseling) between an authoritative and powerful person (a relative or minister) and a person who is vulnerable to and trusting of that power (a child or counselee). Victims often feel responsible for the abuser's activity and so are bound in secrecy by a double burden of guilt and shame."

(3) *God loves you!* In my months of recovery, it was difficult to separate the two—the man who betrayed his sacred trust and God, my Heavenly Father, whom I could trust. To me, the former represented God. However, through my wise Christian therapist, Ann Paxton, I was able to hold on to the *truth—God loved me and I could trust Him.* Because of that, I did not "throw the baby out with the bath water." Yes, I have battled, and continue at times to struggle with cynicism; but my faith in God is strong, and I know he is using that horrible experience to build my character. The story of Joseph is a constant reminder to me of how God can take a heinous crime and turn it into something beautiful and good. Joseph's brothers sold him into slavery, but God used that experience to raise Joseph to a position where he could help his family and the nation of Israel.

(4) *There is help!* As more and more women are coming out of darkness into light and disclosing the "family secret," God is providing help line agencies. Many of these have been started by fellow victims. As he did with Joseph, God is using their painful experiences as a way to reach out to you. Please, dear victim, grab hold of the safety nets God has provided and be set free.

I realize I was fortunate to have an understanding husband who provided immediate support. That will not be the case for many of you. However, if you take a step of faith, I believe God will provide someone in your life who

140

will stand beside you and provide unconditional love and support. Just like we tell children who have experienced abuse, "Keep talking until someone believes you!"

My love and prayers are with you,

Beth Van Dyke

MY FINAL ACKNOWLEDGEMENT

Sean, I know the whole process has been so painful for you. Thank you for not giving up on me. Even from our first date in 1958 to the present, you have helped me believe in myself. I deeply appreciate the emotional support you have given me to start and complete this book. As I wrote, you courageously read and relived the painful events in order to help me remember facts and proofread the manuscript. I will always love you!

To Sean,
my best friend,
You have taught me about God's unconditional love.

IF YOU NEED HELP: YOU MAY CONTACT ME:

Beth Van Dyke
P.O. Box 17442
Irvine, CA 92623-7442
E-Mail address: LNJ2N@AOL.com

CLERGY ABUSE SURVIVOR AGENCIES

CASSANDRA - CLERGY ABUSE SURVIVORS
128 East Olin Avenue Suite 202
Madison, WI 53713
(608)251-5126

CASA - Clergy Abuse Survivors Alliance
5490 Judith Street #3
San Jose, CA 95123
(408)365-7288

CSCA - Connecticut Survivors of Clergy Abuse
190 Norton Ave.
Darien, CT 06820
(203)655-9988

SCAR - Survivors of Clergy Abuse Reachout
264 Avon Beldon Rd.
Avon Lake, OH 44012-1651

SNAP - Network of those Abused by Priests
P.O. Box 438679
Chicago, IL 60620
*(312)409-2720

TAMAR'S VOICE (Advocacy, Support, & Training for Evangelical Survivors)
3130 Crow Canyon Place #260
San Ramon, CA 94583
(510)275-0886

What About Her?

RESOURCE MINISTRIES

<u>CHRISTIANS FOR BIBLICAL EQUALITY</u>
Provides comprehensive biblical scholarship materials
PO Box 7155
St. Paul, MN 55107-999

<u>ISTI - Interfaith Sexual Trauma Institute</u>
Saint John's University and Abbey
Collegeville, MN 56321-2000
(320)363-3931
FAX (320)363-2115
E-Mail isti@csbsju.edu

<u>VICTIMS OF CLERGY ABUSE LINK-UP</u>
1412 W. Argyle, Suite #2
Chicago, IL 60640
FAX (312)334-2292

BOOKS

Fortune, Marie, *IS ANYTHING SACRED*, San Francisco, Harper, 1989.

Grenz, Stanley & Bell, Roy D., *BETRAYAL OF TRUST*, Downers Grove, IL: Intervarsity Press, 1995.

Gula SS, Richard M., *ETHICS IN PASTORAL MINISTRY* Mahwah, NJ: Paulist Press, 1996.

Rutter, Peter, *Sex in the Forbidden Zone*, Los Angeles: Jeremy P. Tarcher, Inc. 1989.

Sipe, A.W. Richard, *SEX, PRIESTS, AND POWER: ANATOMY OF A CRISIS*, New York: Brunner/Mazel Publishers, 1996.

144